APPLAUSE FOR
HOME DESIGN RECIPES

"With her book, *Home Design Recipes*, Cathy transforms the art of interior design into an accessible and digestible feast for the eyes! *Home Design Recipes* offers beautiful, insightful, and delectable design advice, tips, and takeaways that are inspiring and approachable. So...grab a glass of wine, pull up a chair, and dig into *Home Design Recipes*... It's absolutely delicious!"

—**Thom Filicia**, television personality, bestselling author, and founder of Thom Filicia Inc.

"I met Cathy right before she burst onto the national design scene, as a finalist on the reality series, *HGTV Design Star*. She was a star then and remains one of the most relevant and talented designers in the fields of interior design and home staging. Cathy's book, *Home Design Recipes*, is a master class in design!"

—**Ryan Serhant**, real estate broker, television personality on Netflix's *Owning Manhattan* and Bravo's *Million Dollar Listing New York*. Founder of SERHANT. Author of *Brand It Like Serhant* and *Sell It Like Serhant*

"My family has known Cathy personally for nearly four decades. Trust me, she is the real deal—super smart, incredibly talented, and a highly respected expert in the fields of interior design and home staging. Much like having a secret recipe book in your kitchen, giving even beginner cooks the power to create culinary masterpieces, *Home Design Recipes* is an essential must-have for real estate professionals, homeowners, and design enthusiasts alike!"

—**Laila Ali**, former world champion boxer and CEO of Laila Ali Lifestyle

"I know real estate, and I know that design and staging are key to boosting a property's value. *Home Design Recipes* is an essential resource for anyone committed to real estate and design. Cathy Hobbs is a leading expert in the field, and *Home Design Recipes* is chock-full of actionable insights that will guide you to success and sophistication in any space."

—**Barbara Corcoran**, businesswoman, television personality on *Shark Tank*, and founder of The Corcoran Group

"Having known Cathy for more than three decades, I can say she is a true dynamo! I am proud to have witnessed her rise to the top in the field of interior design. *Home Design Recipes* is a 'textbook' in design, capturing Cathy's creativity and expertise, while focusing not only on the 'how' and the 'why' behind effective staging strategies, but the design and showcasing of real estate. Cathy is a true authority in both real estate and design."

—**Amir Korangy**, founder and publisher of *The Real Deal* magazine

"Cathy has managed to tap into two things I love dearly. My home and storytelling. Her unique skills as a former journalist and now as a brilliant interior designer allow her to see the person and not just a space where we live day in and out. In *Home Design Recipes*, she skillfully shares how you can tell your story in your sacred place. That is how I see my home and it is because of Cathy, you will see yours forever."

—**Tamron Hall**, author, television host and executive producer of *Tamron Hall* (ABC Disney)

"Cathy Hobbs is a true visionary in the realm of interior design, and her creation of *Home Design Recipes* has been a game-changer for anyone seeking to transform their living spaces. *Home Design Recipes* is a testament to her expertise and innovative approach to making interior design accessible to everyone. Cathy's keen eye for aesthetics, coupled with her commitment to practical solutions, sets her apart as a go-to authority for creating stunning living environments."

—**Shell Brodnax**, CEO of the Real Estate Staging Association

"Knowing Cathy, I can attest to the effectiveness of her remarkable transformations and approach to design. *Home Design Recipes* distills Cathy's expertise in the fields of interior design and home staging into a format that is not only easy to follow but also enjoyable to explore."

—**Robert Reffkin**, founder and CEO of COMPASS

"Cathy's journey from television news reporter, capturing stories through a lens, to reinventing herself as an interior designer, reimagining spaces with texture, color, and light, is a testament to her vision, determination, and the boundless potential of creative pursuit."

—**Jason Fine**, editor of *Rolling Stone*

"Cathy's extensive journalism background and prolific interior design skills shine in this practical, easy-to-follow, incredibly thoughtful book."

—**Tamsen Fadal**, television personality and bestselling author

"As the founder of one of the largest real estate firms in the United States, I have witnessed a lot of people come and go. Cathy is not only a savvy entrepreneur, but an incredibly talented interior designer and real estate stager. Her book *Home Design Recipes* brilliantly bridges the gap between aesthetic appeal and practical application. Her book is an indispensable resource for real estate professionals and those passionate about personalizing their home environment."

—**Dottie Herman**, vice-chair and former CEO of Douglas Elliman, named "America's Richest Self-Made Woman in Real Estate" by *Forbes*

"I've spent almost twenty years in the vibrant HGTV design world and have seen countless approaches to transforming space. *Home Design Recipes* is an absolute standout because the ingenious room-by-room 'recipes' offer a clear map to beginners as well as pros. *Home Design Recipes* isn't just a great guide, it's an invitation to unleash your creativity and bring your wildest design dreams to life."

—**Kim Myles**, host of HGTV's *Battle on the Mountain* and winner of *HGTV Design Star* Season 2

"In a world where true talent often whispers before it roars, Cathy's voice in interior design is one I've come to greatly respect and admire. As someone who has navigated the peaks of the beauty industry, I recognize the rare blend of passion, innovation, and genuine talent when I see it. Cathy shines both in person and through every page of her beautiful book."

—**Kyan Douglas**, television personality and beauty expert on Bravo's *Queer Eye for the Straight Guy*

"Whether you're a seasoned professional or a design novice, *Home Design Recipes* offers a wealth of knowledge, practical advice, and inspiration to help you achieve stunning results in your own projects and renovations."

—**Stephen Fanuka**, president of Fanuka Inc. and host of DIY Network/ HGTV's *Million Dollar Contractor*

"I have had the pleasure of knowing Cathy since she was a student studying interior design and have watched with pure admiration as she has translated her immense talent to become 'the matriarch of imagination.' I wholeheartedly recommend *Home Design Recipes* to anyone looking to demystify the world of interior design."

—**Joseph Lembo**, owner of Lembo Design Inc., Interior Design Hall of Fame inductee

"From our days on *HGTV Design Star* to now, I've seen Cathy's design talent truly shine. *Home Design Recipes* is the perfect way to cook up unforgettable spaces! She is like the Julia Child of interiors, with each page laying out a recipe for style and simplicity. This book makes design as fun and accessible as cooking a great meal! In the words of Julia Child herself, 'The more you know, the more you can create. There's no end to imagination in the kitchen,' or in the entire house with Cathy's guidance!"

—**Tyler Wisler**, international design expert, finalist on *HGTV Design Star*, and judge/mentor on *The Apartment*

"I love Cathy's *Home Design Recipes*. It provides readers with easy-to-use, step-by-step guides for creating beautiful and harmonious living spaces, and they are the heart of her book. Cathy presents her ideas with such clarity and detail that even those who are completely intimidated by interior design will feel empowered to roll up their sleeves and get decorating!"

—**Evette Ríos**, lifestyle expert, designer, television host, and frequent contributor to *The Rachael Ray Show*

"As an architect, I admire Cathy for her profound impact in the field of interior design. *Home Design Recipes* is a testament to her immense talent, offering both professionals and novices a guide to creating spaces that are as functional as they are beautiful. Cathy's work is not just about design; it's about crafting environments that inspire and endure. Cathy's ability and willingness to openly share her knowledge has inspired many others."

—**Michael Ingui**, president of Ingui Architecture

"With the precision and organization of an easy-to-follow recipe, Cathy's ingenious approach to sharing her vast arsenal of practical design tips breaks down the intricate process of interior design into simple, actionable steps, ensuring every reader can create spaces that resonate with beauty, comfort, and style."

—**Paula Rizzo**, founder of *The List Producer* and bestselling author of *Listful Thinking* and *Listful Living*

"*Home Design Recipes* is more than just a design book; it's a collection of insights and knowledge with universal appeal. Cathy has a gift for making spaces tell stories, for turning houses into homes that reflect the beauty of the people within them."

—**Michele McPhee**, bestselling author, talk radio host, screenwriter

"Cathy Hobbs is not just a talented designer; she's a visionary whose creativity knows no bounds. Her passion for design is infectious, and her ability to transform spaces into stunning works of art is unmatched."

—**George Oliphant**, host and producer of NBC Universal's *George to the Rescue*

HOME
DESIGN RECIPES

HOME
DESIGN RECIPES

Room by Room Recipes for Design

CATHY HOBBS

mango
PUBLISHING GROUP

MIAMI

For permission requests, please contact the publisher at:
Mango Publishing Group
5966 South Dixie Highway, Suite 300
Miami, FL 33143
info@mango.bz

For special orders, quantity sales, course adoptions and corporate sales, please email the publisher at sales@mango.bz. For trade and wholesale sales, please contact Ingram Publisher Services at customer.service@ingramcontent.com or +1.800.509.4887.

Home Design Recipes: Room by Room Recipes for Design

Library of Congress Cataloging-in-Publication number: 2024940108
ISBN: (print) 978-1-68481-629-3, (ebook) 978-1-68481-630-9
BISAC category code: HOM003000, HOUSE & HOME / Decorating & Furnishings

In dedication to my late father, who introduced me to the joy of travel and the concept of goals and dreams, and who always encouraged me to work hard, think big, and never give up. To my mother, who has, with immense pride and joy, always pushed me to believe in myself and wakes up every day excited to hear about my world; from struggles to accomplishments, she is always there to lend advice and wisdom. To my husband, my biggest cheerleader, who tirelessly listens to my ideas and unequivocally believes in me, my goals, and my dreams. To our daughter, whose intelligence, focus, and drive I greatly admire. And to my brother, who sadly knows—yet sincerely appreciates—how the loss of a parent can serve as the ultimate self-motivator for not disappointing oneself or family and is perhaps the one person who truly understands the grit, determination, and decades of hard work that have brought me to the point of being able to author this book.

To travelers, artists, designers, and those who find beauty in the world, in creating, and in imagination.

To fellow workers and dreamers, never forget that "no dream is too big!"

CONTENTS

FOREWORD

In the kaleidoscope of creative professions, paths often cross in the most serendipitous of ways. While my journey has been through the lens of fashion photography, it's the shared essence of artistry and design that brings me to pen this foreword for Cathy's *Home Design Recipes.* Though interior design and fashion may seem worlds apart, at their core, they both celebrate the beauty of expression and the nuanced dance between form and function.

I first became aware of Cathy's work not through the usual professional channels, but through the intertwining of our personal lives, as parents of children attending the same school. It's in these everyday intersections that one often finds the most genuine connections.

Home Design Recipes is more than a mere design book; it is a distillation of Cathy's expansive knowledge, her keen eye for detail, and her unwavering commitment to the spaces we call home. The book weaves together a rich tapestry of themes—from the foundational "design recipes" that lend structure to our creative endeavors, to the pragmatic "takeaway tips" and "design rules" that guide us away from common pitfalls. Cathy's "dos and don'ts" and "top tens" are not just lists, but guides that lead us with simplicity and wisdom through the often-intimidating world of interior design.

As someone who captures moments, I understand the power of a single frame to tell a story or evoke emotion. Cathy, in her own right, masters this narrative within the realm of interior design, transforming spaces into stories, rooms into reflections of one's personality. Her work, much like a well-composed photograph, balances creative elements with precision, ensuring that each space she touches not only looks spectacular but feels individual and personal.

Home Design Recipes is an invitation to explore and experiment. As you turn the pages of this book, I hope you find not only inspiration and guidance but also a kindred spirit in Cathy, who, through her talent and dedication, reminds us all of the transformative power of design.

NIGEL BARKER
Photographer, TV Personality
Judge/Photographer, *America's Next Top Model*, Host, *The Face*

INTRODUCTION

I was never supposed to become a journalist, let alone an interior designer. The two professions never even crossed my mind, growing up first in a suburb of Baltimore and then attending high school in suburban Detroit. It was while attending the University of Southern California that the road map for my professional path began. As a senior in college, I had to make a choice, decide "what I wanted to do with the rest of my life." At the time, I was majoring in business administration, with an emphasis in marketing and finance. The outlook seemed clear enough: graduate, go to work for a big company, become a corporate executive like my father, end of story. As it turned out, the revelation that I wasn't sure that this *was* what I wanted would change my life's path. While watching the evening news one night in my off-campus apartment, it came to me—"I think I want to be a television news reporter!" I quickly applied and was accepted to USC's Annenberg School for Communication and Journalism. I never finished a single class. Just weeks into an introductory newswriting class, I realized I may have made a mistake. We were being assigned obituaries to write when the professor shared that our first job would likely be in the lower rungs of a local newspaper, assigned to write obituaries. But I thought to myself, "I want to be a television news reporter!" Two weeks into the class, the professor—whose name I clearly remember but will omit—pulled me into the hallway and uttered words I will never forget. "I have been in television news for twenty years, and I want to tell you that you will never make it." This is what a professor said to a twenty-year-old! Defeated, I dropped the class and withdrew from the journalism department the next day. Then, it came to me again, "I am not a quitter!" Thanks to the days that predated full computerization, the USC database still showed me as an active journalism student, even though I had withdrawn from the journalism department. I applied for and landed a job writing for the school newspaper, *The Daily Trojan*. From there I wrote article after article on topics students cared about, thus beginning my journey into journalism. That same year, while a senior in college, I landed my first television news reporting job in Bakersfield, California. I graduated from the University of Southern California with a degree in business administration and to this day have never taken a journalism class. I guess you can say I am self-taught. Over a career that spanned twenty years, working in television markets such as Nashville, Washington, DC, and New York City, I earned nineteen Emmy nominations and five Emmy wins. Not bad for someone who was told they would "never make it." I share this part of my journey to say that I have always wanted to help people make easy and attainable what may initially seem hard or impossible.

Home Design Recipes is a compilation of a decades-long journey of creating easy-to-follow recipes for design. As I contemplated having a career Plan B—television news isn't the most stable of professions—I realized I had an interest in interior design. At the age of thirty, while working as an evening television news reporter in New York City, I made the decision to go back to school for interior design. For me, it took seven years to finish a four-year degree. Over eleven semesters, I attended design school at the Fashion Institute of Technology in the morning and then covered "fires and shoot 'em ups" at night; as a nightside reporter, my mornings were my own.

While a design student, I landed my first interior design job designing a friend's kitchen and bathroom. That portfolio led to couples and families hiring me to design their spaces. Around the same time, areas immediately outside of Manhattan, particularly Brooklyn and Queens, captured the attention of real estate developers. After making friends with the real estate agents who sold my husband and me our first condominium, I was quickly hired as the go-to designer/real estate stager for model residences in the incredibly competitive world of new developments. Then in 2011 came a breakthrough moment that would merge my background in television with interior design. While a new mom, I decided to audition for a spot on HGTV's hit reality series, *Design Star*. The premise of the competition-style show was to cast a group of interior designers, assign them a series of design tasks, with the winner getting their own television show. Seemed perfect! For my season, Season 6, more than seven thousand people auditioned for twelve slots. I remember vividly after multiple rounds of auditions, attending the final one. For the final audition, we met with network executives, designed a space, and filled out a detailed questionnaire asking if we knew how to use power tools and equipment. I truthfully replied, "no." My husband, concerned it may prevent me from being cast on the show, wondered if I should have fibbed and replied, "yes." The next day, I was cast on *HGTV Design Star*. I made it through six episodes, winning Episode 5's on-camera challenge.

Today, I own and run an interior design business based in New York City, with our headquarters in New York's Hudson Valley, in which we specialize in real estate staging and styling. We transform blank slates into spaces where people can envision themselves enjoying a certain lifestyle. My interiors are thoughtful, curated, and attainable. For more than a decade, my nationally syndicated *Design Recipes* articles have appeared weekly in hundreds of newspapers. With the book, *Home Design Recipes*, I have carefully assembled a collection of my favorite recipes, with a glorious mix of brand-new ones. Design, create, and be inspired!

With immense gratitude,
Cathy

OUTDOOR SPACES

"TOO OFTEN PEOPLE JUDGE A BOOK BY ITS COVER."

—Cathy Hobbs

FIRE PITS +
HOT TUBS +
OUTDOOR KITCHENS

An outdoor fire pit provides an inviting outdoor oasis.

Whether you live in a year-round warm climate or somewhere that enjoys all four seasons, there are ways to create an outdoor environment that can be just as inviting as your indoor space. Outdoor spaces should enhance, not conflict, and serve as an extension of the design aesthetic one has created indoors.

An outdoor kitchen is the centerpiece of an outdoor entertainment environment.

FIRE PITS

Fire pits are more popular than ever and are especially enjoyable on a chilly night! Fire pits can be either built with the help of a mason or carpenter or purchased as premade, ready-to-use units. In addition to fire pits, there are also fire bowls, which work well for large patios and backyards. When selecting where to place your fire pit or fire bowl, be sure to select a space that is open, and clear of low-hanging trees, to prevent a potential fire hazard.

OUTDOOR KITCHENS

Outdoor kitchens can be basic or elaborate. Begin by selecting the ideal location for your outdoor kitchen. Select a space that will allow adequate room for both cooking and gathering as well as circulation. When designing your outdoor kitchen, you can hire a stone mason or carpenter to build one from scratch or select an outdoor kitchen that is premade. There are also companies that will build a custom, all-in-one unit that only needs to be hooked up with the help of professionals, such as an electrician and/or plumber.

DESIGN RECIPES CHECKLIST

✓ Determine budget

✓ Decide location

✓ Comparison shop

✓ Read reviews

A hot tub is partially built into the side of a hill, creating a dynamic outdoor spa element.

HOT TUBS

Hot tubs remain a popular outdoor amenity and come in different sizes and shapes. When looking to install a hot tub, evaluate how you want it to blend into your outdoor environment. Consider natural screening, such as trees and bushes, as well as a partial enclosure. In selecting a location, find a space that will be accessible and private, and will also blend into your overall outdoor space. One design solution is to install your hot tub first, then enhance the surrounding area with landscaping.

CURB APPEAL

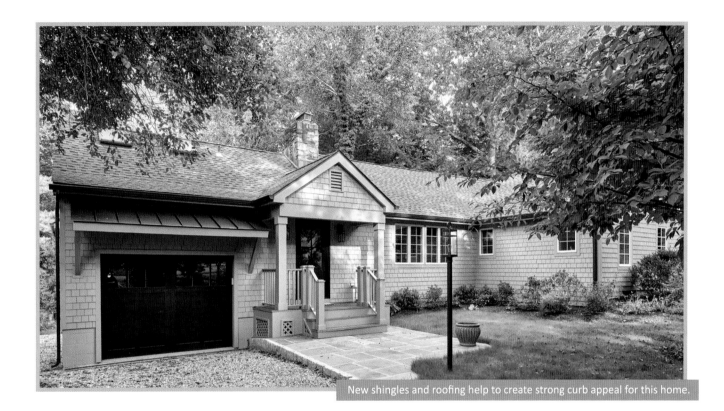

New shingles and roofing help to create strong curb appeal for this home.

A home is often judged both by what is on the inside as well as what is on the outside. First impressions begin with curb appeal as opposed to when someone enters a home. The outdoor aesthetic is often decided by three key elements: the home exterior, landscaping, and lighting.

A colorful mix of landscaping that can be enjoyed year-round fills the frontage of this home.

HOME EXTERIOR

The exterior of a home is often an indicator of what one will experience once inside the home. This is where elements such as design, color, landscaping, and maintenance can play a key role.

> **RULE OF THUMB**
>
> Choose landscaping that will allow for year-round succession of bloom. The goal is to always have some element of your landscape present year-round. Also, consider incorporating plantings into your landscape that will bloom/grow at varying heights.

LANDSCAPING

Landscaping is an investment in the long-term exterior of a home. Many homeowners on a budget often choose to omit or implement minimal landscaping. However, investing in landscaping greatly enhances a home's curb appeal. Begin your journey by visiting a local garden center or nursery. Be sure to bring a site plan of your outdoor space, as well as imagery of your home's exterior. The staff at a local nursery or garden center are often a wealth of knowledge, especially when it comes to native plants and developing an outdoor landscape plan.

LIGHTING

From pathways and sidewalks to a home's exterior, lighting not only is a matter of safety but can also help to enhance the overall look and feel of a home's curb appeal. While hard-wired lighting is preferred and relatively inexpensive to install, these days a variety of solar-powered lighting options can quickly and easily enhance a home's appeal. Lighting can also help to highlight other areas of an outdoor environment such as a home's landscape and hardscape.

Lush landscaping helps to enhance the overall look and feel of this home.

OUTDOOR ENTERTAINING

An outdoor space can easily be transformed into a backyard, balcony, deck, patio, or rooftop entertainment oasis. Amenities such as pools, outdoor kitchens, fire pits, gardens, and outdoor living and dining areas can greatly enhance a homeowner's outdoor enjoyment. Whether you live in a city, suburban, or rural setting, there are several ways to expand the entertainment space of your home by effectively utilizing your outdoor environment.

An organic-shaped pool provides an instant outdoor oasis.

OUTDOOR ENVIRONMENTS

Bringing indoor features, such as kitchens and spas, outdoors remains more popular than ever. Investing in your home's outdoor environment can allow you to expand the perceived footprint of your home and allow the inside to extend outdoors. Creating outdoor appeal may also increase one's sense of calm and allow you to enjoy the outdoor amenities of your home for more months of the year.

CREATING AN OUTDOOR ENTERTAINMENT SPACE

A balcony serves as an urban outdoor entertainment space.

TOP TEN TIPS

1. **Outdoor fire pits:** Fire pits can be made using brick or stone. Outdoor fire pits remain popular because they can be enjoyed year-round.

2. **Outdoor kitchens:** Looking to bring the indoors, out? There is no better way to do that than with an outdoor kitchen, which creates an instant hub for outdoor entertaining.

3. **Pools, spas, and saunas:** While prices can vary relating to cost and maintenance, pools, spas, and saunas remain popular outdoor entertainment amenities. Spas and saunas in most cases are portable, allowing you to move them to a different home or location if needed.

4. **Pool and tree houses:** Not just child's play, these outdoor living spaces can be used for both entertaining and lounging.

5. **Outdoor living spaces:** Think of your backyard as an outdoor living room by making the space feel as comfortable as possible, infusing everything from outdoor sofas and area rugs to coffee tables and chairs.

6. **Outdoor dining:** There is something quite appealing about dining alfresco. Set up a dining zone that is separate from your living zone. Options include rectangular or round tables in addition to more modern, highboy seating.

7. **Gardens:** Not only do gardens add to the overall appeal of an outdoor space, but a garden can also add lots of interest and color as well.

8. **Sun protection:** From trellises to covered patios and umbrellas, sun protection may play an important role.

9. **Outdoor children's entertainment:** Outdoor entertainment shouldn't be solely for adults but the entire family. From basketball hoops, trampolines, and swing sets, there are several ways to keep every member of the house happy and entertained.

10. **Outdoor fabrics:** When looking to incorporate outdoor upholstered seating, outdoor fabrics will add to their longevity.

An urban rooftop all decked out for the perfect party.

THE ESSENTIALS

First and foremost, think about décor, how you wish the party to look and feel as far as style and theme, then determine the colors you wish to use.

Themes can help to enliven a party tablescape.

DECORATIVE ELEMENTS

Parties are always a wonderful time to showcase your creative skills as well as some of the decorative party items that you've kept tucked away in cabinets. From plates and napkins to decorative trays, candles, or condiment holders, consider elements that can add a creative, decorative element to your table.

3 Fs

The 3 Fs help to make your party truly come to life: food, fun, and family and friends. Food and beverage are really the cornerstone of any great party. The next F, fun, is your opportunity to entertain your guests, with backyard games, music, poolside fun, or great conversation. Lastly, family and friends, this may be the most important of all, enjoy your guests!

Lush native landscaping in full bloom.

NATIVE LANDSCAPING

Native landscaping is part of a trend relating to outdoor environments in which the installed landscape is indigenous or native to a particular geographic environment or region. What this typically allows for is a landscape that not only blends more organically with its surroundings but often requires less pesticides to maintain.

TOP TEN TIPS

1. Conduct research to learn which plants are native to your area or region.

2. Select a landscape specialist with knowledge of native landscaping.

3. Visit a local nursery to gather information and ask questions.

4. Evaluate your soil to determine the ideal location for planting.

5. Have a water system in place. You will want to avoid areas that accumulate excess water.

6. Create a landscape plan first, then plant.

7. Select plantings that allow for succession of bloom or year-round foliage.

8. Choose a sunny location for your landscape.

9. Incorporate plantings that will grow to different widths and heights.

10. Look to blend color, shape, and size into your native landscape.

Naturally grown succulents.

DESIGN RECIPES OUTDOOR CHECKLIST

In general, several maintenance tasks can preserve the look and efficiency of your home, while also helping to provide peace of mind.

QUICK MAINTENANCE REMINDERS

- **Tree maintenance.** Be sure to keep an eye out for dead trees as well as low-hanging limbs and branches.
- **Insect control.** Protect your home and plants from unwanted visitors.
- **Driveway re-paving.** Severe weather can cause damage.
- **Water connections.** Ensure no leaks at locations such as outdoor kitchen faucets, showers, and garden hoses.
- **Windows and doors.** Ensure proper caulking and sealing to reduce energy loss.

ENTRIES + FOYERS

"AN IMPRESSION IS MADE, EITHER POSITIVE OR NEGATIVE, WITHIN THE FIRST THREE SECONDS OF ENTRY INTO A HOME."

—Cathy Hobbs

SENSE
OF ENTRY

Mirrors placed upon entry help to instantly open a typically small space.

FIRST IMPRESSIONS

Foyers and entries serve as the "greeting point" in any home. They should be inviting and welcoming as they also create a first impression for guests. The first impression should be strong and impactful, while also being functional. Begin by taking a step back, placing yourself into the role of being a guest, and take in what you first experience upon entering the home. Allow this experience to serve as the roadmap for your design.

A black-and-white color story is introduced upon entry into a brownstone-style home.

DESIGN RECIPE **DOS AND DON'TS**

Dos

Do create a clear point of entry; this can be done by having an entry console, bench, or wall décor such as an oversized mirror or piece of art.

Do look for ways to incorporate bold pieces of art to view upon entry.

Do incorporate greenery when possible, such as trees or plants.

Do consider a wall feature such as mirrors or wallpaper upon entry.

Do create a color story upon entry into your home, introducing a color scheme in a foyer or entry.

Don'ts

Don't ignore creating an entry that is also functional. For example, a table to place keys, or a sitting bench.

Don't create a décor element in an entry or foyer that is not in keeping with the overall décor of your home.

Don't overstuff or over-clutter an entrance or foyer. Clean and minimal is best.

Don't ignore lighting in the entry or foyer. Consider an interesting pendant or chandelier.

Don't engage in multiple finishes or textures in an entryway or foyer. Often, one can view multiple parts of a home from an entrance. The décor and color message should be cohesive.

A black-and-white photograph makes a bold statement upon entry into a Manhattan loft.

DESIGN RECIPES TAKEAWAY TIPS

- Benches in an entry or foyer can provide both a design element and function.

- Artwork in an entry or foyer can allow for a bold design statement and "wow" factor.

- Mirrors help to lift and brighten an entry space.

- Case goods such as sideboards and consoles can help to make large spaces feel grounded.

- Add lighting such as pendants, table lamps, and chandeliers to help to brighten foyers and entries.

MAKING A BOLD STATEMENT

A message upon entry can be warm and welcoming, bold and bright, or functional and inviting. Regardless of the message you want to convey, look for opportunities to introduce a sense of style and creativity while also making a memorable first impression.

A sense of elegance and grandeur is introduced through a blend of art, mirrors, and décor in this foyer.

DESIGN
BY NUMBERS

An entry sideboard displays a vignette of decorative items.

There is often a rhythm and cadence to design just like with other creative mediums. With design, typical questions involve the dilemma of groupings. For example, should items be placed in pairs? Is there truth in the "power of threes"? The answer is that both can work well, in addition to a series of odd or even groupings that, in interior design, are often referred to as "vignettes." Using pairs and groupings is a method of placing décor that involves "design by numbers."

An entry wall displays groupings of decorative mirrors and frames.

DESIGN RECIPE **DOS AND DON'TS**

Dos

Do consider hanging art in a series, such as two pieces in a series, known as a diptych, or three pieces, known as a triptych.

Do repeat a rhythm or pattern in a space. For example, various groupings of odd-numbered elements.

Do mix and match various elements in a grouping to help add interest, color, and texture.

Don'ts

Don't place items without thought and purpose.

Don't overcrowd a space with too many elements as to not overload the eye with an abundance of décor.

Don't ignore the power of repetition such as repeating a décor element, color, or pattern in a space to create cohesion.

Two is the magic number in this entry when it comes to artwork, mirrors, and décor items.

DESIGN RECIPES TAKEAWAY TIPS

THE THEORY OF NUMBERS

Pairing more than one item or identical items in a group essentially provides the eye with visual reinforcement. The most successful techniques often involve the grouping of identical or similar items.

PAIRINGS

The use of pairings, or two identical items or similar items placed together, is one of the few instances where it doesn't overwhelm if used multiple times within the same space. The pairing of similar art pieces, two identical lamps on top of two identical end tables, for example, helps to create cohesion without being too overpowering.

THE MAGIC OF TWOS AND THREES

Twos and threes are the most common groupings in home décor. Typically, they are utilized when accessorizing decorative selections such as a pair of mirrors, series of art pieces, or similar or identical décor items placed side-by-side. Additionally, the same can involve larger items such as side tables, chairs, sofas, and even area rugs. Grouping identical or similar items together helps to create cohesion, as well as serving to visually trick the eye.

Three identical accessories, of different sizes, are placed in a series on an entry sideboard.

PORTABLE
DESIGN

An entry sideboard displays a vignette of decorative items.

Portable design is one of the best and easiest ways to transform a space, swapping out the old and bringing in the new. Portable design is represented through those pieces that can be lifted and transported from room to room and home to home. Portable design done well can also allow you to prolong your décor, by allowing you to repurpose and reuse much of what you may already own.

Portable décor elements including artwork and accessories make a bold entry statement.

TOP TEN TIPS

1. Mirrors. Mirrors whether leaning or hung are great portable décor items.

2. Artwork. Whether you purchase artwork to fit a space or just want to add interest, artwork is both a functional and useful portable décor item.

3. Lighting. Fixtures don't always have to remain permanently installed in a home. Have a fixture you love? When it comes time to move, consider swapping it out and taking it with you.

4. Area rugs. Whether you are looking to move an area rug from room to room or home to home, area rugs are excellent portable décor items.

5. Benches, ottomans, and chaises. These pieces can be placed floating in a space or against a wall and work well in entries and foyers.

6. Books and accessories. Books and small décor items are perfect to display on shelves and entry consoles.

7. Small furniture pieces. Furniture such as side tables and chairs are easily movable portable design pieces.

8. Greenery. Whether real or artificial, florals, plants, and trees are useful portable décor items.

9. Inspiration. Choose a strong inspirational piece of art to serve as the centerpiece of your design and create a "wow" factor.

10. Entries. Don't feel that you must overcrowd or overwhelm. In most instances, "less is more."

A simple color scheme of black, indigo, and white.

MATERIALS

GLASS

Glass consoles are ideal for those areas where the entry may be small or narrow. Glass will automatically help a smaller space feel more open without making the point of entry feel overwhelming or stuffed.

WOOD

Wood is versatile and an ideal material for those who seek timeless elegance. If you are looking for a more formal and elegant look, wood can help provide a luxurious feel. Conversely, if an industrial vibe is more to your taste, wood can also be an attractive choice.

PORTABLE DESIGN TIPS

- Select a color palette that includes a maximum of three colors.

- Select furniture of the appropriate size and scale.

- Use neutral colors to not overwhelm.

- Consider incorporating mirrors to help make the entry space feel bigger.

- Add a case good such as a console or sideboard to help make the entry feel more grounded.

- Utilize vignettes and groupings of decorative elements. A grouping of three is common.

- Add seating such as a bench or chairs to help create a sense of entry.

A wood console adds texture and interest.

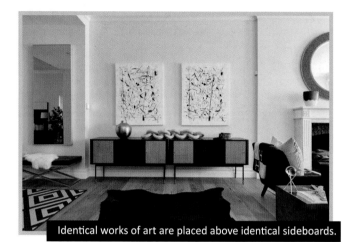

Identical works of art are placed above identical sideboards.

QUICK DESIGN RECIPE

- Select a focal point in your entry to introduce the concept of rhythm and repetition.

- Utilize identical selections such as artwork or accessories to help create a harmonious sense of rhythm and repetition.

- Maintain a sense of balance using elements that may be of different height and weight but blend well together.

- Consider infusing patterns or graphics into your entry space, using artwork.

- Use a neutral color palette as a foundation as this will allow for the best way to build a color palette.

RHYTHM AND REPETITION

Just like the right music or tempo can enliven the words of a song, rhythm and repetition can help to establish the appropriate tone and mood in design. One can set a rhythm and utilize repetition in a variety of ways, including colors, shapes, and materials.

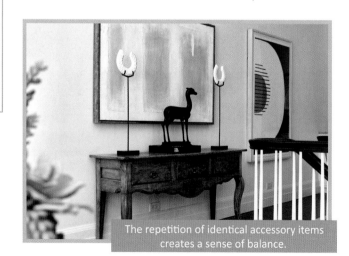

The repetition of identical accessory items creates a sense of balance.

The hallway is elongated and highlighted using artwork and mirrors.

QUICK DESIGN RECIPE

- Select a bold or inspirational piece that makes a strong statement.

- Use elements such as mirrors to create a sense of openness.

- Choose furniture that is smaller in scale such as consoles and benches.

- Incorporate colors in hallways that are cohesive with your overall color scheme. Use color as a connector.

- Avoid making hallways overly personalized. Instead use them as ways to extend your design style.

HALLWAYS

From the initial point of entry to passageways, hallways serve as visual connectors in a home. Often ignored or overlooked, hallways can serve as a key design opportunity to unify or extend one's color palette and overall design aesthetic.

What are some ways to highlight your hallways? To begin your hallway design story, start with the moment of first impression or point of entry and then build upon your design vision.

HALLWAY DÉCOR OPTIONS

Mirrors	Shelves	Benches
Artwork	Consoles	

A series of mirrors helps to reflect light in a hallway.

KITCHENS

"WHEN IT COMES TO DESIGN, DON'T IGNORE THE KITCHEN, OFTEN CALLED THE 'HEART' OF THE HOME."

—Cathy Hobbs

WHITE
KITCHENS

White cabinets with frost glass inserts help to provide storage as well as privacy.

When considering creating a new kitchen or renovating an existing one, what is the best color to select when it comes to cabinets? These days, more than ever, the answer is the color white. White is a popular and desired choice for homeowners looking to create a timeless and elegant look that also creates a neutral and appealing color palette.

White cabinets paired with ebonized wood floors add an interesting sense of contrast.

A CASE FOR WHITE CABINETS

- White cabinets blend well with a large variety of countertop and tile choices.

- White cabinetry is versatile and neutral and won't clash with existing furniture and furnishings.

- White cabinets can shine regardless of the hardware finish, from chrome to nickel and brass.

- White cabinetry is timeless and elegant.

- White kitchen cabinetry remains a popular and desired choice as it relates to home resale value.

DECORATING WITH WHITE

White is one of the most misunderstood colors. With infinite shades, white is often a difficult color to match. Even so, the color white is one of the most versatile, especially for those looking to create a monochromatic, neutral color palette. White not only works well with other colors, but its tints, tones, and shades also can help to create a strong sense of contrast when paired with other colors.

White marble countertops and backsplash are paired with white cabinetry.

White cabinetry paired with stainless steel appliances.

DESIGN RECIPE **DOS AND DON'TS**

Dos

Do pair white with warm elements such as wood.

Do use white in kitchens with lots of windows, as white helps to bounce light.

Do use white complementary elements such as backsplashes and countertops or furnishings such as barstools.

Do use white to create a sense of contrast when paired with darker colors such as indigo, chocolate brown, and black.

Do repeat white throughout your kitchen.

Don'ts

Don't worry about color matching. It's OK to blend different shades of white.

Don't mix too many shades of white that are tinted, such as white with hints of blue, gray, and green.

Don't ignore the power of layering and repeating shades of white throughout a space.

Don't use white excessively in a space as it can potentially lead to a less elegant look.

Don't ignore the element of using artwork or white-framed mirrors to add hints of white to your color scheme.

HEALTHY
DESIGN

An organized cabinet with plates and bowls displayed through a glass front.

Many desire one's home to feel like a haven, a place where you feel warm, cozy, and safe. Health is also top of mind, creating an environment that is both clean and healthy. As you look for ways to beautify your environment, there are several ways to ensure clean design, creating visually appealing spaces that are both environmentally friendly and beautiful.

An organized industrial-style kitchen.

Greenery and herbs can help to infuse fragrance into a kitchen.

TOP TEN TIPS

1. Remove shoes upon entry into your home to prevent tracking outdoor pollutants indoors.

2. Wash and/or launder items such as floor mats or textiles as much as possible to help keep your environment clean and fresh.

3. If possible, switch from carpet to hardwood, especially in key areas such as entries and hallways leading in and out of a kitchen.

4. Consider making your own cleaners—lemon juice and water is a fantastic cleaner as well as baking soda and vinegar.

5. For kitchen surfaces, select nonporous materials, such as quartz and porcelain, that are also easy to clean and maintain.

6. Wash sponges or replace them frequently. You can place sponges in the dishwasher to clean them. This will help to reduce the spread of germs.

7. Deep clean. Deep cleaning one's kitchen on a regular and consistent basis will help to maintain a healthy environment.

8. Open the windows. There are so many benefits from allowing fresh, clean air to help ventilate your home from time to time.

9. Incorporate greenery to help circulate oxygen throughout your home.

10. Wash and/or replace dishtowels frequently.

**DESIGN RECIPES
TAKEAWAY TIPS**

SCENT

Scents can almost instantly bring a sense of calm to a space. Scents can also linger, which will help to extend a sense of freshness and cleanliness.

Lemons displayed on a kitchen counter help to add a fresh scent.

NATURAL SCENTS

Fresh Lavender. Lavender is a wonderful scent for the home. Place lavender in gauze spice bags (available in any grocery store in the spice aisle) or in open jars to help release the scents.

Eucalyptus. This natural plant packs a powerful, appealing aroma.

Rosemary and Mint. These traditional herbs are wonderful when placed around the home in creative ways.

Fresh Lemons or Limes. Citrus scents provide a fresh, clean, and affordable way to add an appealing aroma to your environment. Squeeze fresh lemon or lime in water for floating candles or freshly cut flowers or simply have them on display.

ORGANIZATION + STORAGE

Kitchen items are concealed within full-height cabinetry in this modern kitchen.

When it comes to organizing the kitchen, it can be a work-in-progress, an evolution that can take place over time. Even so, the foundation of creating a kitchen that is functional and provides ease of use is rooted in basic design elements.

DESIGN RECIPE **BACK TO BASICS**

Organization begins with basic design recipe rules.

THE ABCDs

A

ALPHABETIZE AND ARRANGE

Grouping similar items together will go a long way toward creating an orderly kitchen. Beyond grouping similar items together, you can also create a color-coding system or arrange items in alphabetical order.

B

BOXES AND BINS

Boxes and bins can instantly organize the kitchen. The essence of an organized kitchen prep and work environment is to have "a place for everything and everything in its place."

C

CONTAINERS AND CABINETS

Containers, especially those that are clear with lids, can be the perfect choice for loose items such as spices, flour, and sugar. Cabinets also allow for multi-level storage. When looking for ways to maximize storage, be sure to order extra shelves so that you can really maximize your vertical space.

D

DIVIDERS, DRAWERS, AND DOORS

A kitchen with lots of drawers allows for easy access and ease of use. Dividers can really help organize and separate items, and doors help to keep items tucked away.

TOP TEN TIPS

EASY+ AFFORDABLE KITCHEN ORGANIZATION HACKS

1. Use tension rods to help divide and store cutting boards.

2. Use magazine holders to organize foils, wraps, cutting boards, or even canned goods.

3. Use short mason jars, plain glass jars from the hardware store, or office supply containers to store spices.

4. Use a Lazy Susan. Being able to rotate items is always a plus.

5. Use a pocket or shoe organizer to hold cleaning supplies.

6. Use stacked PVC tubing to store wine bottles.

7. Use drawer inserts for multiple storage uses around the kitchen.

8. Use wire baskets for storage. They allow for transparency and can work in both modern and country settings.

9. Use a peg board to hang pots or other kitchen items such as utensils.

10. Use a dish drainer as an organizer for plastic storage lids.

Mason jars are used for both decoration and storage.

Inexpensive bottles from a discount store can be used to store oils and other liquids.

RENOVATION DOS AND DON'TS

Kitchen Renovation Before.

Kitchen Renovation After.

Dos

Do obtain multiple bids. Regardless of whether it's love at first sight, having multiple bids may also help to provide peace of mind, knowing that you didn't overpay for your renovation.

Do ask for previous samples of work or references. This will help to ensure that your hired professional has executed similar renovation projects.

Do have inspirational images and a sense of your overall design direction. There is nothing worse than flying blind in a renovation project.

Don'ts

Don't purchase your materials after your project has commenced; instead try to have fixtures, appliances, and finishes preordered to avoid delays in your project which will likely increase the cost.

Don't submit change orders or try to submit as few as possible, as most contractors charge additional fees.

Don't micromanage. While it is prudent to be on top of your project, it may be counterproductive to be overly involved.

Open shelves are blended with closed cabinetry in this modern kitchen.

ALTERNATIVE CABINET SOLUTIONS

SHELVES

Shelves can be used for various purposes whether decorative or to serve specific functions. When most people think of shelves, kitchens likely come to mind. In kitchens, storage is at a premium and creative use of shelves and shelving can add interest, function, and pizzazz. From metal, wood, and lacquer, shelves can be both affordable and purposeful.

Stainless steel shelving helps to create an industrial vibe.

BATHROOMS

"A BATHROOM SHOULD BE SO CLEAN AND TIDY AS TO LOOK LIKE IT IS RARELY USED."

—Cathy Hobbs

VANITIES +
CABINETRY

A well-crafted bathroom vanity is paired with nickel hardware to create a timeless look.

Pedestal sinks are out, and cabinets and vanities are in. At least if one is looking for additional bathroom storage. In larger spaces, vanities and cabinetry can provide much-needed countertop, drawer, and storage space. Beyond allowing for more storage, vanities and cabinetry provide the opportunity for an elevated level of craftsmanship and customization that can enhance the beauty and overall luxury of a bathroom space.

Custom cabinetry provides a modern feel in this bathroom.

DESIGN RECIPE **DOS AND DON'TS**

Dos

Do select cabinetry made of solid construction.

Do consider the cabinetry interior configuration in determining desired function and need.

Do keep in mind that cabinetry will get wet from time to time.

Do consider cabinetry alternatives to wood.

Do focus on color when considering the ideal vanity or cabinetry.

Don'ts

Don't forget to measure your space prior to ordering a vanity or cabinetry (especially when it comes to custom selections).

Don't overlook the possibility of using professional services such as a bathroom specialist or design showroom.

Don't mix too many different materials and colors in a small space.

Don't use materials that could warp or become damaged in high-moisture conditions.

Don't ignore the opportunity to incorporate custom cabinetry such as utilizing the skills of an artisan, carpenter, or millworker.

A fully renovated bathroom with custom cabinetry allows for a bespoke look.

A natural stone countertop is paired with walnut cabinetry.

COUNTERTOP MATERIALS

- Natural stone
- Solid surface
- Porcelain or ceramic
- Laminate
- Concrete
- Quartz

A custom countertop is integrated with an overall aesthetic using natural stone.

DESIGN RECIPES TAKEAWAY TIP
COUNTERTOPS

Beyond your vanity and cabinetry choice exists the selection of the ideal countertop. The countertop material selection will not only play an integral part in the overall look and feel of a bathroom but also, depending on usage, how the surface will perform and last over time.

BATH
BASICS

Accents and accessories help to make this bathroom feel warm and cozy.

They are often ignored or discarded spaces. But bathrooms regardless of size can be a source of calm and an opportunity for design. Where do you start? While renovations can make for the perfect project, they are often costly to take on. There are several ways to spice up your bathroom without breaking the bank, by incorporating "bathroom basics."

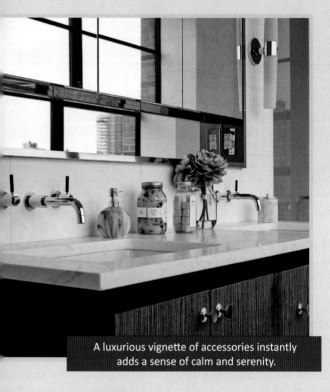

A luxurious vignette of accessories instantly adds a sense of calm and serenity.

TOP TEN TIPS

1. Bring the outdoors in. Greenery is a great place to start. From trees to plants, bringing in greenery can help create a sense of calm.

2. Include natural elements. From stone to sand and even natural elements such as wood, integrating organic elements can help to create a sense of serenity.

3. Add pops of color. Flowers and succulents are great ways to integrate color and texture.

4. Hang artwork. Walls don't have to be bare and boring. Artwork can help to add color and a sense of whimsy.

5. Make a statement with tile. Whether it's a border, a small pattern, or overall coverage, tile is one way to make a bold statement in the bathroom.

6. Add windows to your bathroom space. The light can truly help to elevate these small spaces.

7. Go big! Big mirrors and large walls of mirrors reflect light and can make these small spaces feel bigger.

8. Paint! From an accent color to overall coverage, paint brings in color and interest.

9. Add luxury elements. Bathrooms can truly integrate a sense of calm. From bath salts to oils and candles, go for it!

10. Create a sense of space. Creating a bath that is separate and distinct from a stand-in shower remains a trend and the preferred design of architects and interior designers.

Windows help to add light and openness to a Manhattan bathroom.

DESIGN RECIPES RULES
DOS AND DON'TS

Dos

Do make your bathroom a functional space in your home. Ideally bathrooms should not be used for storage, cleaning products, or supplies and should feel fresh, open, and airy.

Do utilize florals. While fresh flowers are ideal, in many instances it simply is not feasible. An attractive artificial arrangement will do the trick.

Do incorporate color into your bathroom, a pop of color can go a long way.

Do have a fresh set of towels hanging on a towel bar or ring. In a guest bathroom especially, many guests may be turned off by the idea of using towels that you and your family may have also used for bathing.

Do infuse fresh fragrances into your space. Diffusers and candles can also help to add color and instill appealing aromas.

Don'ts

Don't make bathrooms an afterthought. Guests will certainly not feel welcome in a space that does not feel clean and fresh.

Don't ignore the opportunity to include artwork in bathrooms. Artwork helps to add interest especially in small spaces such as guest bathrooms.

Don't only prepare a powder room or guest bathroom for guests. Ideally, any bathroom in the home, outside of a master suite, should always be "guest ready."

Don't ignore lighting. A well-lit bathroom is always more appealing.

Don't overdo it. Many bathrooms tend to be small, so be sure not to overcrowd your space.

FIXTURES + FINISHES

Satin nickel fixtures add timeless elegance to this bathroom.

Fixtures and finishes, if selected purposefully, can serve as the crown jewels in a bathroom space. Fixtures and hardware, as well as finish selections, can play a prominent role in the overall aesthetic look and feel. Use a certain finish or style of fixture or hardware and a space may feel traditional and elegant, while another fixture and hardware selection in an alternative finish may make the same space feel modern and luxurious.

Copper is often used for its look as well as its heat and cold retention properties.

MIX + MATCH

Choose a specific style that suits your space and maintain this consistent style throughout your bathroom environment. It is OK to mix and match materials when looking to create interest.

SELECTING A FINISH

A finish should complement as opposed to conflict with your bathroom space.

COMMON FINISHES

Nickel • Chrome • Brass • Oil Rubbed Bronze • Copper • Black

FINISHES

Fixtures typically come in several finish options such as polished, brushed, and matte.

A bathroom filled with an abundance of natural light.

LIGHTING

A well-lit bathroom is always more appealing.

WAYS TO INCORPORATE LIGHT

Windows • Sconces + hanging pendants • Ceiling fixtures • Skylights

Hygge focuses on infusing a sense of calm and tranquility.

DESIGN RECIPE
SOOTHING ELEMENTS

Bring softness into your space. Hygge, in essence, means bringing warmth and coziness into the home; décor elements such as thick towels and rugs are the perfect way to achieve a sense of hygge.

Light a candle. The Danish love candles, from candle-making to interesting ways to display candles. Lighting candles will help to provide a sense of hygge by creating a soothing environment while also bringing in a welcoming fragrance.

Invoke thought. Hygge is also about a sense of mindfulness. One way to achieve this in the home is by incorporating insightful elements such as expressive or interpretive art.

Wood accents and greenery. Taking inspiration from nature is a creative way to incorporate hygge.

RECHARGE + REFRESH + RENEW

Unplug from electronics. Reading is a preferred activity, as opposed to watching television or using computers and electronics.

Clear the clutter. Minimalize. One aspect of hygge also relates to what is often referred to as "silent design," in which as much excess as possible is removed from one's home or tucked away.

Think white. White is a popular foundation color in Denmark, helping to create a clean, calming sense of serenity and hygge. The color is often used for furniture, fixtures, appliances, and flooring.

Eco-friendly design helps to create a healthier environment.

DESIGN RECIPES TAKEAWAY TIP

Do your homework.
Several respected national and international organizations certify green products. Among them, the UL GREENGUARD Certification Program evaluates and certifies products based on strict chemical emission standards, and Green Seal, an independent global nonprofit organization, certifies green products.

ECO-FRIENDLY TIPS
GREEN IS THE NEW BLACK

Green is the new black. In home décor, it is on trend and increasingly the go-to choice for those looking to rejuvenate their home and be healthier at the same time.

QUICK DESIGN RECIPE

GREEN TIPS

- Use low or zero VOC paint.
- Switch to low-flow toilets, shower heads, and faucets to conserve water.
- Switch light bulbs to compact fluorescent or LEDs.
- Buy a programmable thermostat and lower thermostat setting by five to ten degrees.

LIVING ROOMS

"LIVING ROOMS SHOULD PERFORM DOUBLE DUTY, DESIGNED FOR RELAXATION AND ENTERTAINING."

—Cathy Hobbs

SOFAS

A well-constructed sofa serves to anchor this living space.

For many, a sofa is a once-in-a-lifetime purchase or at least a purchase infrequently made. The longevity and quality of a sofa, in most cases, relates to what you can't see: how a sofa is constructed and made.

A sectional sofa works well to help frame a space.

DESIGN RECIPE **SOFA TYPE**

Sectional or traditional sofa, with arms or armless? While there are plenty of choices, allow your room or space to be your guide. In general, sectional sofas work well when looking to frame a space or room using furniture. Sectional sofas work particularly well in corners or where one is looking to frame a wall. Look for components that fit your desired usage. For example, a chaise would be a better choice than an ottoman when creating a sectional component for lounging.

CONSTRUCTION

Sofa frames are made in different ways (machine versus by hand) and how a sofa is made, depending on its usage, may play a key factor in how long it will last. In general, nothing beats all-hardwood construction. A sofa constructed of low-grade wood or particle board simply will not last as long as one that is made from solid hardwood. Also, look for sofas in which components such as legs are made of either solid wood or metal. Another key component is ensuring that springs or coils are well-made, and that the sofa frame construction components are well-cushioned and wrapped, prior to upholstery. For those looking for increased durability, a popular designer choice is to select commercial- or hospitality-grade fabrics that repel liquids and stains while still being attractive and aesthetically pleasing.

An upholstered sofa made of heavy-duty fabric.

Fabric-covered sofas can pair well with both fabric and leather chairs.

CUSHIONS

Foam versus down. If you prefer a stiff or firm look and feel, then foam is the way to go. However, if you enjoy a more relaxed look and love the feel of sinking into a sofa, then opt for sofa cushions filled with down.

MATERIALS

Fabric versus leather? Cotton versus velvet? Sofa materials have a whole host of options, especially relating to fibers and alternative material options. Ask questions and be sure to ask a manufacturer or retailer for cuttings or swatches before making a purchase. Not crazy about fabric? Leather is still a popular option, especially in areas that may be used by children, or a home inhabited by pets. Looking for an alternative to leather? Artificial leathers remain popular and come in myriad textures and colors.

COMMON SOFA MATERIALS

Velvet	Artificial Leather
Cotton	Microfiber
Leather	Polyester
Wool	

Leather remains a popular and timeless choice.

MID-CENTURY
MODERN

A mixture of dominant mid-century inspired pieces makes a bold statement in a Manhattan loft.

Mid-century modern design is more popular than ever. Is it making a comeback? Or has it never really gone away? Whether you want a modern, minimalist look or a space that is classic and timeless, mid-century modern design may be the ideal design aesthetic to help make your space shine.

An industrial-style New York City residence incorporates various mid-century modern pieces.

TOP TEN TIPS

1. Consider incorporating shag or sheepskin. These high-texture textiles can be used instead of traditional area rugs.

2. Choose bold, colorful graphic prints when looking to make a statement with art.

3. Look to acquire classic mid-century modern pieces like dining tables and chairs.

4. Incorporate metals and finishes into your space, such as brass, which remains the go-to mid-century modern finish.

5. Consider using black-and-white prints in place of traditional artwork.

6. Go for both matte and shine. Lacquer comes in all levels of shine. Both matte and high gloss can be used when looking to achieve a mid-century modern vibe.

7. Bring in the wood. Wood pieces and those made by artisans are great ways to infuse mid-century modern design into a space.

8. Go industrial. Many industrial pieces also lend themselves to a mid-century modern aesthetic.

9. Consider leather. Leather or artificial leather are durable choices with mid-century modern décor.

10. Be creative with color. Beyond classic colors such as black and white, consider other colors when it comes to leather, such as butterscotch or saddle brown.

A classic-style, mid-century modern side chair adds a timeless element to a living space.

DESIGN RECIPES TAKEAWAY TIPS

WOOD

Look for wood elements. Wood can help to achieve an instant mid-century modern vibe.

CLASSIC DESIGN

Purchase classic or vintage elements that are authentic to the mid-century design aesthetic.

Create elements of warmth through portable design elements, such as toss pillows and throws.

Think neutral. Neutral colors such as taupe, cream, and soft gray can help to create a soothing, calm, mid-century modern vibe.

TEXTURE

Consider textured materials for upholstery pieces, such as bouclé, neutral cotton, and velvet.

ART +
MIRRORS

Three pieces of artwork in a series (triptych) are placed with a pair of identical mirrors.

Mirrors can be used for both function and decoration. They can also serve as a focal point in a space, to help make rooms feel larger, reflect light, and serve as a visual alternative to artwork. Meanwhile, artwork can provide the foundation for the design direction in a space, helping to infuse color, graphics, and texture.

An oversized round mirror provides a key focal point in this living room.

MIRRORS **TOP TEN TIPS**

1. Consider leaning mirrors as an alternative to those that are wall-hung.

2. Go big. Larger mirrors help to fill space.

3. Consider the unexpected, such as a mirror that is antique or ornate.

4. Try hanging mirrors in pairs or in a series.

5. Use mirrors in spaces that don't receive much light.

6. Experiment with mirrors made of different materials or finishes.

7. Utilize mirrors to highlight architectural elements like fireplaces.

8. Try unexpected shapes such as squares.

9. Mix artwork with mirrors within the same space to create interest.

10. Use mirrors in areas where you want to add a sense of depth, such as a hallway.

A gallery wall displays framed art of various sizes.

ARTWORK **GALLERY WALLS**

When it comes to displaying one's treasured art pieces and mementos, in many instances, homeowners are electing to embrace the unconventional. Enter the gallery wall. Gallery walls remain an interesting—if not dramatic—design display tool in which groupings can be displayed in an interesting way.

RULE OF THUMB

Most people make the mistake of hanging artwork too high. The center of a piece of artwork or framed photograph should be at eye level, which typically is defined as five feet above the finished floor. Artwork should be hung approximately six inches to one foot above furnishings such as sofas, sideboards, and consoles.

DESIGN RECIPE **TOP TIPS**

Repeat. Repeating the same or similar items together can create a cohesive and interesting display.

Mix items of a different color or material. It can appear whimsical and inviting to utilize those pieces you love.

Go bold. Creating a display that spans a whole wall can make a statement.

Try mirrors. Mirrors are ideal elements to display in a repetitive way.

Use vignettes. Vignette groupings can create an aesthetically appealing gallery display.

Create a pattern. Pre-plan the location of the items you wish to display before putting a single nail in the wall.

A narrow living room is enhanced using proper furniture placement.

FURNITURE PLACEMENT 101

One of the biggest challenges when it comes to setting up one's space relates to how to properly place furniture. Knowing the basic elements of spatial design and common floor plan configurations will help to serve as a guide.

ROOM SHAPES
Rectangular • Square • Angled • Curved

DESIGN RECIPES RULES
PLAN FIRST. THEN PURCHASE.
Measure your space, both the width and length and, if needed, the height.

Obtain measurements for your desired furniture. Nearly all furniture selections will provide product dimensions.

Plan and sketch. Plan out your space on paper. This step isn't about drawing ability, but serves as a helpful visualization tool.

Furniture is placed in this living room using a straight-furniture layout.

DESIGN RECIPES TAKEAWAY TIP

Go modular. Modular furniture pieces allow for the most amount of flexibility, furniture arrangements, and configurations.

TYPICAL FURNITURE LAYOUTS

STRAIGHT

This type of furniture arrangement works well when furniture is mostly arranged along a single long wall.

PARALLEL

This furniture arrangement works well in narrow rooms where furniture groupings are placed opposite each other.

ANGLED

This arrangement can work well when space is challenging as angling helps to maintain a space's openness.

L-SHAPED

This popular arrangement helps to frame a space while still allowing for an open feel.

Coffee tables showcasing two sets of vignettes.

DESIGN RECIPES CHECKLIST

✓ Use groupings of twos and threes
✓ Pair similar colors + materials
✓ Incorporate surprise elements

VIGNETTES

Design isn't always about the big pieces in a room, sometimes it is the smaller, specialty pieces that can make a room shine. Often this is greatly influenced by what pieces are selected and how various objects are placed or grouped together. Enter the vignette. Vignettes are a grouping of similar or dissimilar objects that, when placed together, look harmonious and appealing and help to enhance the overall look and feel of a space.

WHAT MAKES A GOOD VIGNETTE?

A vignette is essentially a snapshot or mini grouping of items to convey a design message. A vignette can be a grouping of furniture items and accessories, such as pillows, or tabletop items, such as sculptural pieces, vases, or even flowers.

QUICK DESIGN HACK

Build a vignette around an inspirational or dynamic piece and make this item the focal point of your vignette.

A long sideboard displays a grouping of cohesive yet distinctive accessories.

TOP TEN TIPS

Vignettes placed on coffee tables help to enhance this modern living room.

Objects of various heights help to add interest and dimension.

1. Group decorative elements in pairs or sets of three. This provides a nice rhythm for your décor.

2. Create vignettes of similar colors. Monochromatic color schemes can be modern and fresh.

3. Infuse metallic elements to help create a sense of luxury.

4. Include surprising elements that will help make a vignette feel unique.

5. Create vignettes from harmonious but dissimilar elements to allow items to feel cohesive, yet different.

6. Use vignettes as an opportunity to bring in color and texture.

7. Include florals and greenery in vignettes to add both color and texture.

8. Use vignettes as an opportunity to showcase your favorite finds or unique mementos.

9. Use bookshelves and shelving as ways to display vignettes. Also consider including books as vignette elements.

10. Use objects of varying heights to add interest to the eye.

A small side table vignette.

FAMILY ROOMS

"THESE TYPES OF ROOMS ARE MEANT FOR ONE TO ENJOY THE 3 Fs: FOOD, FUN, AND FAMILY."

—Cathy Hobbs

MODULAR
DESIGN

A family room is made long and spacious using a modular sofa.

Whether you are looking for versatility or to create a unique configuration, modular furniture has become a popular go-to for interior designers. Gone are the days of a one-size-fits-all approach. Enter modular, in which a room can be framed, or a seating arrangement created from sections as opposed to a single unit. Modular configurations are especially popular in urban areas where elevator sizes may prohibit some furniture options, but they are also gaining favor with those who simply desire a more customized seating approach.

Modular sofa sections allow the greatest amount of flexibility.

DESIGN RECIPES TOP TIPS

THE SPACE

Evaluate and measure the space you are looking to design, taking into consideration pathways and room flow.

FLEXIBILITY

Select modular pieces that are armless or have features such as reversible sections or removable arms. These flexible selections allow the largest variety of configurations from the same modular section.

FABRIC CHOICES

Purchase modular furniture pieces in solid-colored fabrics to avoid having to worry about matching a pattern or design.

WHAT TO AVOID

Avoid sections that have connectors. It is best to have sections that are fully upholstered on both sides to maximize flexibility.

A modular sofa utilizing three sections.

Modular pieces of artwork can be used instead of one large piece of art.

ART OF MODULAR DESIGN

There are multiple ways within a space in which to utilize aspects of modular design. The art of modular design revolves around the principles of individual units or modules that work harmoniously together or when separated as standalone parts.

WAYS TO INCORPORATE MODULAR DESIGN

DESIGN RECIPES TAKEAWAY TIP

Sofas

Coffee Tables

Artwork

Side Tables

WARM
COLORS

Toss pillows and colored barware help to infuse a sense of warmth in this family room space.

Brrr...even when it isn't cold outside, one way to warm up your space is with color. Warm colors help to add a sense of coziness and warmth to a space. From warm oranges to reds and yellows, warmer tones can help to transform a space that may be cold and cavernous to one that is warm and inviting.

Warm colors are repeated throughout this family room to create a warm and cozy feel.

DESIGN RECIPE DOS AND DON'TS

Dos

Do use black. Black is not only a warm color, but one that is neutral and can instantly add warmth and depth to a space.

Do incorporate color and warmth through your use of artwork. Infusing color and warmth using art can really help to warm a space and adds a finishing touch.

Do use small decorative items such as books and florals to bring warmth and color into your home.

Do mix warm tones together such as yellow, orange, and red. The result can be appealing and cozy.

Do use metallics. Brass remains one of the hottest finishes in home décor right now and is a wonderful way to incorporate warmer tones into any room of the home.

Accents and accessories are often overlooked as an opportunity to infuse color and warmth.

DESIGN RECIPE DOS AND DON'TS

Don'ts

Don't overwhelm a space with too many warm colors as it may appear to be overly dark or muddy. Instead sprinkle warm accents throughout the room.

Don't paint ceilings dark, warm colors as this will instantly close in a space and make any space feel smaller. Instead, the ceilings should be light and bright, preferably white.

Don't forget accessories. Accessories are an easy and affordable way to infuse warmth into nearly any room.

Don't use too many wood pieces in the same room. Too many opaque elements, such as wood, will add visual weight to a space. Instead, consider mixing heavier wood pieces with those that are lighter or translucent, such as pieces made of acrylic or glass.

Don't forget to use mirrors. Mirrors are one of best ways to open a space and can serve as a key design element. These days frames also don't have to be generic in nature. Instead of using a plain frame, why not use one that is painted in a warm color or trimmed in a warm-toned metallic finish.

TEXTURE + TEXTILES

A variety of tactile and textured materials fill this family room space.

Texture and tactile materials can infuse an often-ignored sensory element: touch. How often have you enjoyed how something felt to the touch? Perhaps you were inspired by a furry pillow, textured throw, or thick area rug. Incorporating texture into your space can help to both elevate your home and please the senses.

Velvet pillows of different colors and sizes help to infuse texture into a family room.

TOP TEN TIPS

1. Use toss pillows as an opportunity to bring in texture. Materials such as velvet and even some cottons are good places to start.

2. Throws, throws, throws. Throws are portable, come in various colors and materials, and can be a wonderful way to infuse texture.

3. Consider faux fur. Faux fur remains a popular way to bring texture into a design space.

4. Wall art can be the ideal way to incorporate texture in an innovative way.

5. Textured, shag, and raised area rugs can instantly help bring in a textured element.

6. Textiles such as drapery can provide a finishing touch to a space.

7. Consider upholstery as an opportunity to infuse texture.

8. Small furniture elements such as benches and ottomans can be used to infuse texture.

9. Consider wood and organic elements in areas where you wish to incorporate texture.

10. Greenery such as flowers and plants can add a textured element to nearly any space.

Texture is infused through brightly colored artwork, as well as an oversized fabric chair adorned with a fabric toss pillow.

TEXTURE

Texture is a key and often ignored or overlooked element in home décor. From tactile materials to elements such as fabric, wood, and metal, texture can greatly enhance nearly any space and provide a room with an instant pick-me-up!

AREA RUGS

Area rugs top the list of ways to add texture to a space. From flat weaves and thickly knotted to those that have raised elements, adding an area rug to a space will instantly help a room feel warm and cozy while also incorporating texture.

FAUX FUR

Faux fur is still a popular way to add both texture and a cozy element to your home.

WOOD

From a piece of furniture to decorative elements such as trays, side tables, and accents, wood is a wonderful way to add texture to a space.

METAL

From brass to chrome and other finishes, metal adds a sleek, smooth texture to a room as well as color and an element of glam.

FABRICS

Whether it is the upholstery on a sofa, chair, or toss pillow, fabric is a great way to add texture and tactile elements to a room. Materials such as leather, wool, velvet, and even certain cottons can add texture to a space.

Playrooms can be divided into zones for a variety of activities.

CHILD-FRIENDLY COLORS

Curious about child-friendly colors? One can seldom go wrong with a mix of warm, cozy colors, such as brown and deep orange, or those that are brighter and cheerier, like mustard yellow or a crisp green. Dark colors will go a long way as far as concealing spills and stains, while bright, friendly colors serve as a great contrast to dark colors and help to create an inviting environment for a child. Be sure to use neutral colors as your base palette so that you can transform or renew the same space as the children get older, simply by swapping in different colors.

ADDED FUN

Lastly, playrooms don't necessarily have to be expensive. Invest in some key games, sturdy furniture, and a quality television for viewing. From there, some of your other pieces can be less expensive, such as items that are repainted, refurbished, or repurposed from another area of the home.

PLAYROOMS

Let's face it: for kids, it's all about having fun! Children need an engaging environment in which to play, enjoy themselves, and be a kid. First and foremost, I suggest that you divide your proposed children's area into various activity zones.

Begin by creating a movie or video game zone that works as an area for gaming and movie watching. Then, create a separate board game zone for traditional board games. And finally, a flexible activity zone. This is an area that can be used for anything, from train sets to dramatic play and puppetry to arcade-style games or even a ping pong or pool table.

Creating different zones helps to create a floor plan that will best utilize your space and will also ensure that multiple children will be able to enjoy themselves and be engaged for long periods of time.

A pair of leaning mirrors flank either side of a fireplace mantel.

FIVE FAVE TIPS

- Select a stone, material, or finish that will enhance, not detract.

- Pay attention to color, size, and scale.

- Incorporate an anchor element to help ensure a fireplace stands out, such as an oversized mirror or artwork.

- Utilize design principles such as symmetry and balance.

- Consider placing mirrors on either side of a fireplace as an alternative to placing mirrors above.

FIREPLACE DÉCOR

Fireplaces both keep us warm and serve as a decorative focal point and highlight in a home. Whether you are looking to showcase an ornate fireplace mantel or create a cozy seating area, being thoughtful and purposeful with one's décor and style choice can help to maximize the experience for you and your guests.

QUICK DESIGN RECIPE DOS AND DON'TS

Dos

Do place furniture in a cohesive way to highlight the fireplace as a focal point.

Do place mirrors above or next to a fireplace to help draw the eye and reflect light.

Do consider replacing, painting, or adding a decorative mantel.

Don'ts

Don't block the path to a fireplace or crowd it with too much furniture.

Don't be afraid to paint existing stone or brickwork.

Don't place a television above a fireplace if possible. Electronics may detract from one's décor.

HOME OFFICES

"**THERE SHOULD BE A DISTINCT PLACE IN A HOME FOR WORK THAT IS SEPARATE AND, IF POSSIBLE, PRIVATE.**"

—Cathy Hobbs

SMALL
ROOM
SECRETS

A simple yet well-designed and functional workspace.

Small spaces come with their own challenges. One challenge is, of course, square footage, while another is often function. To unlock this design dilemma, the key is to make a small space have a clear and distinct purpose, function, and use. Whether your workspace is a wall or an entire room, design and function should still play a prominent role. In designing the ideal work environment, think of its function first and then let design be your guide.

A narrow workspace is enhanced using mirrors and creative furniture placement.

A small workspace is created in a second bedroom.

TOP TEN TIPS

1. Define the type of work you wish to do in your work environment.

2. Think about function first. Ask the question, do you need a private or shared workspace?

3. Ask yourself how you want your work environment to make you feel. Consider colors, mood, and atmosphere.

4. Add personal touches, such as family photographs or personal mementos.

5. Add plenty of light, especially since a work environment is used during different parts of the day.

6. Choose a space with good natural light and fresh air.

7. Hire a professional for special technical needs, if necessary, such as connectivity.

8. Select a quiet space to avoid disturbing others or being disturbed by outside noise or distractions.

9. Choose colors that speak to your personality. Fill your workspace with colors that enliven you.

10. Design your work environment to feel cozy, by including elements like artwork, area rugs, and accents.

Energy colors such as yellow and orange help to add pops of color to this home office.

CREATING A SENSE OF AT WORK CALM

TAKE A BREAK

Take frequent breaks during the day. Once in the morning, around lunch, and before the end of the day is ideal.

HEAD OUTDOORS

Spend some time outdoors. Taking time for a breath of fresh air will help instill a sense of calm.

INFUSE SOOTHING OR ENERGIZING COLORS

Infuse soothing colors to create a sense of calm. Pure white, neutrals, and soothing blues can help. Looking for a more energizing environment and feel? Choose citrus colors such as yellow, orange, and red to help to add energy and warmth to your work environment.

APPEAL TO THE SENSES

Consider incorporating scent or fragrance. A calming effect can come from soothing the senses.

LIGHT IT UP

A workspace is enhanced using natural light.

Let there be light! Lighting often plays a critical role in enhancing spaces and molding moods whether the environment is one for relaxation, sleep, or work. From decorative, ambient, and task lighting, many homeowners may ask, "Does my home have enough light?" Often there is a general rule of thumb: whenever possible, try to utilize as much natural light as you can, perhaps adding windows or doors to a room, or bouncing light using mirrors or transparent surfaces such as acrylic or glass to allow more natural light to enter a space.

A workspace is illuminated through task lighting.

TOP TEN TIPS

1. Decide what mood you wish to create and illuminate a room accordingly.

2. Create multiple light sources in larger spaces, such as a table lamp, floor lamp, and ceiling pendant.

3. Utilize task lighting, such as a reading lamp.

4. Consider placing some of your light fixtures on dimmers, allowing for different levels of illumination.

5. Purchase fixtures that require multiple bulbs, as this will automatically increase the output of the fixture.

6. Use high-wattage light bulbs.

7. Don't overdo it! There is nothing worse than seeing a space cluttered with too many floor or table lamps.

8. When possible, add recessed lighting.

9. Select energy-efficient bulbs or LEDs. Energy efficiency is always preferred.

10. Illuminate hallways, pathways, and stairwells that lead to your home office. It's a matter of safety!

A windowless home office is designed to feel warm, cozy, and well-lit.

LIGHTING WINDOWLESS ROOMS

From lack of natural light to functionality and feasibility, windowless rooms pose a unique challenge.

LIGHTING OPTIONS

PORTABLE LIGHT Table and floor lamps.

FIXED LIGHT Recessed lighting, pendants, chandeliers, and wall sconces.

STRUCTURAL LIGHTING Clerestories, dormers, or skylights.

MIRRORS

Mirrors can help widen a windowless space, add a sense of spaciousness, and give the illusion of windows.

DÉCOR AND DESIGN TRICKS

- Incorporate light elements such as light-colored paint and neutral fabrics.

- Incorporate interesting design elements such as wallpaper or a bright paint color.

- Be purposeful with furniture as windowless rooms tend to be smaller spaces.

- Incorporate floor coverings to help make windowless spaces feel cozy.

WORKSPACES

A workspace designed with colorful design elements such as accessories and artwork.

With so many people working from home, one challenge may be in how to create an adequate and productive work environment, especially if more than one adult is working in the household. The goal should be to plan and design your home-office environment creatively and purposefully to produce a work environment that is bright, fresh, and productive.

Shelves and bookcases can help to make workspaces feel less cluttered.

QUICK DESIGN RECIPE

HEALTH TIPS

Ventilate your space periodically throughout the day. Fresh air goes a long way in creating a healthy environment.

ERGONOMICS

Choose a comfortable work chair. While workspaces and desks are important as far as comfort, a comfortable work chair should also top your list.

ORGANIZATION

Try to store documents away from your work surface when possible. Keeping your work area neat and tidy will also help to keep the creative juices flowing!

GREENERY

Bring living elements such as plants and trees into your work environment. Greenery will help bring life to your space as well as serve to circulate oxygen.

DESIGN RECIPES RULES GETTING STARTED

FINDING SPACE

Ditch the guest bedroom. So often guest bedrooms go unused except for just a few times a year. Why not turn every room of your home into a productive space? Guest bedrooms make for the ideal home-office space.

CREATE

If possible, create your home office in a room with a window. Natural light in several ways plays a role in creating an inviting and productive work environment.

COLORS

Integrate colors that you love into your space. Does orange make you happy? Does blue make you calm and relaxed? Color can often play a role in creating the right mood and tone in your space.

PRIVATE VS. SHARED

Try to create a separate workroom for your home-office space. Depending on your home environment, additional privacy may be needed.

SPACE-SAVING TIPS

Challenged with space? Consider creating your workspace in a currently occupied area of your home, such as a bedroom, or incorporating a space-saving solution, such as a slim or convertible piece of furniture, like a table that transforms into a desk.

A small nook off a master bedroom is made into a functional home-office space.

A home office is made homey and inviting through the repeated use of texture and textiles.

LIFE + WORK BALANCE

As the dynamics of home and work converge, there is often a desire to separate the two. How do you avoid home feeling like the office and ensure you are still creating an environment that feels like home? The design recipe lies in creating an ideal blend of work and relaxation under the same roof.

CREATE A WORK ZONE

Create a separate area for work. Ideally this should be a separate room, but if you can't, create a work zone that is separate and distinct from an area used for activities such as sleep, relaxation, or play.

INCORPORATE NATURE

Try to incorporate nature and natural elements, such as wood and wood-like items and fixtures. This can help to ground a space and help to make it feel cozy.

INFUSE LIGHT AND AIR

When possible, utilize natural sunlight or infuse as much light as possible into your workspace. Sunlight can help to calm the mind.

TEXTURE + TEXTILES

Try to make your home-office environment soothing and calm. From textures and textiles to colors that make you feel calm, feel free to transform your space into an oasis.

Shelf dressing is a way to incorporate design elements and small décor.

SHELF DRESSING

From built-ins to portable shelving like bookcases, often there is a design dilemma relating to the best way to dress shelves. There is, in fact, an art to shelf dressing, a rhythm that can be created and repeated, through a thoughtful selection of accessories.

DESIGN RECIPE DOS AND DON'TS

Dos

Do be very thoughtful and careful with your selections, as opposed to choosing items randomly.

Do look for similar colors, finishes, and tones.

Do incorporate elements such as greenery and blooms to help add interest and texture.

Do use bins and baskets when looking to fill larger areas on shelves.

Do use books as filler. A popular shelf dressing technique is to pair books of similar height and color together.

Don'ts

Don't be afraid to use contrasting colors. Dark items on a light-colored shelf, for example, can provide an inviting sense of contrast.

Don't overdo it. Less is more.

Don't forget that shelving can also be an opportunity to highlight a curated selection of collectibles.

Don't be afraid to create empty space. Intentionally leave certain shelves bare to create a visual sense of rhythm.

Don't overlook interesting ways to create shelving, such as found, repurposed, or reclaimed materials like wood.

DINING AREAS

"THE JOY OF ENTERTAINING TAKES PLACE IN A DINING SPACE REGARDLESS OF THE SIZE."

—Cathy Hobbs

TABLES + CHAIRS

A mix of dining chairs creates interest in this dining space.

It is often said that the kitchen is the heart of the home, where a family gathers as well as entertains its guests. An extension of this is one's dining space. These two areas of the home lend themselves to specific needs relating to gathering, aesthetics, and functionality. When it comes to dining spaces, these days, many homeowners may also desire flexibility. From size, shape, and materials, there are several options to evaluate and consider when selecting both tables and chairs for your space to dine and entertain guests.

A glass dining table helps to make a dining space feel open and airy.

DESIGN RECIPES TAKEAWAY TIPS

TABLES

Tables come in all shapes and sizes as well as finishes. The first place to start should be size then shape.

TABLE SELECTION

Measure your space to determine the footprint needed for your table.

Evaluate what size would work best. Typical shapes include rectangular, oval, round, and square.

Select your desired table material based on durability, design, aesthetics, and budget.

MATERIALS

WOOD

Wood is a great choice when looking for durability. From tables that are intended for more formal dining rooms to those that are made by artisans, you can't go wrong with wood.

LACQUER

Lacquer is a popular choice for a modern, sleek vibe. Lacquer can also allow one to integrate unique or custom colors into a space.

GLASS

Glass is an ideal choice for smaller spaces as its transparency instantly allows a space to feel open and airy as opposed to closed in.

A round table maximizes the space in a small dining area.

SHAPES

ROUND
In smaller spaces, oval or round tables allow for increased circulation and flow.

SQUARE
Square tables work well in small environments such as studio apartments or when looking to seat small groups of two to four people.

RECTANGULAR
Rectangular tables are ideal for roomy dining spaces and to accommodate larger groups.

SHOPPING HACKS FOR DINING CHAIRS
DOS AND DON'TS

Dos

Do buy chairs for comfort.

Do buy one to two extra chairs in case one gets damaged, and you are unable to source.

Do source locally when possible.

Don'ts

Don't purchase chairs in fabrics or materials that are hard to clean or can become easily soiled or damaged.

Don't ignore durability elements such as frame material and solid construction.

Don't purchase chairs in odd numbers, instead think of purchasing as a set or grouping.

TRADITIONAL
TOUCHES

The use of lighting helps to create a timeless and elegant feel in this dining space.

Modern, sleek décor isn't for everyone. For many, a touch of formality or traditional elements is the height of luxury. Creating a traditional feel doesn't have to overwhelm or feel outdated. Touches of tradition can be elegant and elevate a space to feel timeless versus trendy.

An elegant chandelier adds a sense of grandeur to this dining space.

DESIGN RECIPE DOS AND DON'TS

Dos

Do blend old with new, pairing antiques with more modern elements.

Do source locally. Your local antique store, flea market, artisan craft fair, or estate sale can be sources for traditional furniture and furnishings.

Do incorporate heirlooms or pieces that have personal or sentimental meaning.

Do consider adding one-of-a-kind or unique elements, such as original murals or artwork.

Do use furniture elements with traditional details like nail heads and tufted upholstery.

Don'ts

Don't cover up or conceal original details. Highlight historical elements such as original wood.

Don't ignore traditional finishes such as marble and granite when looking for finishes that will feel timeless.

Don't use elements that are considered dated or old-fashioned.

Don't oversaturate a room with too much color. Muted, understated tones often feel more traditional and elegant.

Don't ignore the power of mirrors. Large mirrors can help make a room feel large and airy and can also be used as a focal point and key design element.

Grass cloth wallcovering adds an element of texture in this dining space.

WALLPAPER

What goes around comes around especially as it relates to style and trends. Wallpaper was once a staple and standard in the '70s, then fell out of favor in the '90s, but in recent years has made a comeback. No longer automatically considered tired and dated, many décor companies have tried to design fun, bold prints that can add texture and drama to a space and help to make a statement.

QUICK DESIGN RECIPE

DESIGN RECIPES TAKEAWAY TIPS

Consider using wallpaper for an accent wall.

Use colors in your wallpaper pattern as the inspiration or springboard for your color story.

Consider removable wallpaper as an alternative to traditional wallpaper.

Frame wallpaper as art. This is a popular design trick especially with large-scale prints.

Consider texture. Grass cloth as well as beaded or fabric wallpaper is also an option.

Consider overscale patterns when looking to select a statement wallpaper.

141

CENTERPIECES

An organic table arrangement helps to add a modern feel to this dining space.

Gone are the days of formality and keeping the table set. What's in are tabletop décor items that are functional, aesthetically pleasing, and, in some instances, unexpected and colorful. Creative tabletop décor is the modern trend in styling that, for many, serves as an extension of how they wish to live and present their home to guests.

A modern centerpiece arrangement with succulents and moss.

DESIGN RECIPE
DESIGN RECIPES TAKEAWAY TIPS

ARTIFICIAL FLOWERS

Artificial florals were once taboo, considered unattractive dust collectors. Now, they are popular with weekend and vacation homeowners, as well as those who desire no-maintenance, colorful floral solutions. When choosing silk florals, consider arrangements that are both large and small; in fact, small single-bloom arrangements may have the biggest impact.

SUCCULENTS AND MOSS

At first glance, artificial succulents often don't look much different from the real thing. Succulents are an attractive and modern way to decorate and pair well with items such as sand, stone, moss, and grass.

ORGANIC ARRANGEMENTS

Instead of only choosing a traditional floral arrangement, why not consider one that is organic and unique? Selections such as bamboo, branches, topiary, and plants and flowers that mimic those found in nature are popular choices.

A DIY arrangement helps to add a sense of whimsy to a modern dining space.

DIY ARRANGEMENTS
DESIGN RECIPES PROJECT

CHOOSING A VESSEL

The first step is to select the right vessel for your arrangement.

Pottery   Glass
Ceramic vases   Wood
Bowls

GREENERY AND FLORALS

When choosing what to use for your arrangement, consider both color and texture.

Blooms   Branches
Succulents   Leafy stems

Moss works well to add a finishing touch.

FILLER AND FINISH DETAILS

Foundation and finishing elements will help your arrangement look complete and cohesive.

Moss   Sand
River stones   Leaves

A dining space includes both a kitchen island as well as a dining area that is an extension of the kitchen.

ISLANDS

Islands help to enhance a home in several ways. Not only do islands help to define a space, but they also serve as additional work surfaces. Many families desire to create numerous dining experiences, from casual to seated to formal dining areas. Islands allow one to add bar stools to create a functional bar-style dining experience.

EXTENDABLE TABLES

Designers love using extendable dining tables because of their flexibility. Gone are the days of complicated table leaves that must be removed and stored away. Instead, many furniture manufacturers are making dining tables that include simple lift-and-slide features, so tables can expand and extend to one's needs.

EAT-IN SPACES

Eat-in spaces tend to be more casual but need to be highly functional. When creating the ideal eat-in experience, ask yourself these questions: "Should the table be round or rectangular?" and "Should the table be expandable?" Materials are also important: Glass tables create a sense of lightness, while solid surfaces like wood provide weight. For corner spaces, consider a round table to allow for increased visual flow. Depending on your space, benches or banquettes may also work.

Accents of black in the lighting, artwork, and centerpieces add a luxurious look.

BEAUTY OF BLACK

Look inside nearly any shelter publication and you will see the color black in virtually every room of the home. Black is a color that can instantly add a sense of luxury and elegance. Black is a power color that you shouldn't be afraid to use in any room you desire. Black can be used as an accent color for a wall, a base color in the form of an area rug, or the color of your primary furniture pieces.

QUICK DESIGN RECIPE

WHY BLACK?

Black is a color that is often overlooked. Neutral, bold, and luxurious, black can be used as an accent, a pop of color, or to make an overall statement.

ARTWORK

Artwork is a great way to introduce or tie various colors together within a space.

AREA RUGS

Area rugs come in different shapes and sizes, as well as various color combinations that can help you introduce black into your home.

ACCESSORIES

Accessories allow for interesting and creative ways to introduce black into your space.

"MASTER BEDROOMS SHOULD FEEL LIKE A SANCTUARY: INVITING, RELAXING, SOOTHING, AND SPECIAL."

—Cathy Hobbs

BEDROOM
ESSENTIALS

Soothing neutral tones provide a sense of luxury in this master bedroom.

When it comes to selecting the perfect décor for your bedroom, it doesn't have to be about spending lots of money, but about creating a soothing and calming atmosphere that reflects your personality and creates the ideal oasis.

In refreshing your bedroom, remove excess pieces and keep those pieces that you love, using them as inspiration to create an overall décor story or as the foundation for your master bedroom color palette.

Layers of relaxed bedding helps to create a feeling of softness and sumptuousness in this master bedroom.

DESIGN RECIPE FIVE FAVE TIPS

NEUTRAL BEDDING

Select neutral bedding. It will serve as the perfect blank slate for you to build a bedroom color palette. After selecting your bedding, add color and texture through your artwork and accessories.

TOSS PILLOWS

Buy colorful, nicely patterned toss pillows. Toss pillows will provide you with an affordable way to update the look of your bedroom, quickly and easily. Think about swapping out toss pillows seasonally for a fresh new look!

SHEETING

Invest in great sheets. A popular choice is cotton in a 400 thread count or higher. Looking for a bit of glam? These days, sheeting often includes embellishment such as embroidery or a decorative border pattern.

ESSENTIAL FURNITURE

Purchase the essentials. Must-have essentials include a well-constructed bed, nightstands, decorative table lamps, and a dresser with a beautiful mirror above.

SCENT

Layer a scent. Soy-based candles and scents such as lavender can help open your senses and refresh your mind. Place fresh lavender in tiny cheesecloth pouches and scatter them throughout the bedroom to infuse scent into your space. Diffusers are also an ideal way to infuse a continuous aroma.

DESIGN RECIPE SPLURGE VERSUS SAVE

SPLURGE

SLEEP PILLOWS

Memory foam versus down, soft versus firm, based on sleep position; a sleep pillow should be a thoughtful choice.

TYPES OF SLEEP PILLOWS

Down and down alternative
Feather
Memory foam, latex, or gel

FOUNDATIONS

Foundation or mattress. This is a prime area where you will want to splurge. A mattress should be selected with great care in person, and, if possible, should include seeing, touching, feeling, and lying on the product.

BEDS

When choosing a bed, look for sturdy and strong materials with quality craftsmanship and joinery. In the case of upholstery, consider materials such as leather or stain-resistant fabrics.

SAVE

FITTED SHEETS

Many designers recommend using two flat sheets as opposed to a fitted sheet paired with one that is flat. When using two flat sheets, the top sheet should be one size larger than the mattress size.

DUVET INSERTS + COVERS

Often one can find value-priced options in this vast category.

TOSS PILLOWS

Toss pillows are a designer's secret weapon, which you can purchase without breaking the bank. Together, outdoor pillows used indoors and purchasing affordable covers and inserts make for some cost-saving hacks.

A layered bed includes elements such as sleep pillows, toss pillows, duvet covers, coverlets, and decorative blankets.

CLOSET
ORGANIZATION

Built-ins allow for items large and small to be organized and hidden.

Clear the clutter! More than ever, people are opting for minimalism versus overstuffed and cluttered. Whether it's a small closet or a large walk-in, organization is often the key to productivity and maximizing space. One philosophy relates to the rule: *everything should have a place and be in place.* Closet organization begins by asking yourself some key questions:

> When was the last time I wore this item?
> Does it still fit?
> Does it need mending?
> Does it have a stain on it?

All these questions can help you to decide if an item is something you should keep or something that should go!

The organization of accessories and shoes helps to improve the tidiness of a closet.

TOP TEN TIPS

1. Purchase bins, boxes, baskets, or containers to store small items.

2. Label. Labeling is a key organization tip. One of the best solutions is to use erasable labels.

3. Color code. Color coding will help you more easily identify items.

4. Hide the small stuff. Often it is not the large items that cause disorganization, but the smaller items that less easily find homes. Store small, similar items together.

5. Create both open and hidden storage. Shelves work great for displaying shoes or folded clothing, but you will also want to have closed, hidden storage as well for those items that you don't wish to be visible.

6. Follow the *one in, one out* rule. When you get a new item, discard or donate an older, outdated similar item.

7. Inventory. Oftentimes, items are boxed away in an attic or basement never to be seen or heard from again. At least once a year, take inventory of what you have, what you need, and what you can toss.

8. Minimize. Ask yourself: "Do I really still need this?" Typically, if you haven't used it in a year, the answer is "no."

9. Utilize clear storage solutions. Clear bins and containers allow you to see what you have and use what's inside!

10. Purge! Each season get rid of something that can go to a new home!

DESIGN RECIPES RULES

Custom millwork helps to create a finished and well-organized closet.

CLOSET ORGANIZATION HACKS

Use a drawer utensil divider to organize jewelry.

Use kitchen cabinets to create order and organization in closets.

Buy a multi-drawer toolbox. You can use these to organize everything from jewelry to beauty supplies.

DESIGN RECIPES TAKEAWAY TIPS

Unwrap dry cleaning. If you can see an item of clothing, it is easier for you to remember it is there and wear it!

Use huggable hangers instead of those made of wood. They reduce space and keep your closet orderly.

Fold clothing and place both in- and out-of-season items in clear bins, labeling the outside of the bin with a marker. Quick hack: for specialty items, place a photo of the item on the outside of the bin.

Use erasable boards, then purchase erasable markers for labeling.

MODEST BUDGET

If you are on a modest budget, consider just adding shelving and bars for clothing, as cabinets and drawers are more intricate and costly.

MEDIUM BUDGET

These days, many retail stores offer various ready-made, off-the-shelf organization and cabinet options. If possible, meet with an in-house professional and take advantage of their design and measuring services.

READY TO SPLURGE

If budget isn't an overwhelming concern, then built-ins are the way to go. Built-ins allow you to customize. This process often involves a custom millworker or cabinetmaker creating shop drawings and then building cabinetry to order. A millworker or cabinetmaker will also properly install cabinetry for you.

BEDMAKING 101

Layering makes for a sumptuous bed.

Beds are meant to be comfortable, inviting, and luxurious. For some, dressing the bed is an art form, involving an array of pillows, texture, and lots of layers.

A well-dressed bed creates a feeling of luxury and tranquility in this master bedroom.

DESIGN RECIPES RULES

CREATE A MOOD

How do you want your bedroom space to make you feel? Do you want the space to feel warm and cozy or cool and tranquil? Whatever you choose, you want to make the correct selections to help set the right balance. Warm colors will make a space feel cozy, while cool colors will create a feeling that is both tranquil and calm.

SELECT A DESIGN AESTHETIC

Modern or traditional? What is your aesthetic? Knowing your own personal style and desires will provide direction as you select the perfect bedding. Traditional? Look for soft fabrics and small, simple prints. More modern? Think of clean elements, such as piping or stripes, or go bold with graphic prints.

MUST-HAVES

Where does one get started? When creating the ideal bed, think of layering. Essentials include sumptuous sheets; a good-quality, quilted coverlet; followed by a high-quality, well-made cotton duvet cover with a thick duvet insert; finished with a blanket or throw placed at the foot of the bed.

DESIGN RECIPES TAKEAWAY TIP

Many designers recommend using flat sheets as opposed to a flat and fitted sheet. Top flat sheets should be one size larger than the mattress size to allow them to be sufficiently tucked around the mattress.

THE ANATOMY OF BEDMAKING

FROM THE BOTTOM TO THE TOP

THE LAYERS

- Mattress

- Feather bed (if a softer bed is desired)

- Mattress cover

- Bottom fitted sheet or oversized flat sheet

- Top sheet

- Coverlet or blanket

- Duvet cover (with duvet insert inside)

- Throw and toss pillows to add a pop of color or texture

- Sleep pillows (typically stacked in pairs)

Elements like piping or embroidery can add an elegant touch to one's "top of bed."

Texture and pattern can make an unexpected, yet impactful design statement.

HEADBOARDS

Headboards are sometimes viewed as inexpensive alternatives to a bed ensemble that includes side rails and footboards, but headboards can also provide an opportunity for creativity and even saving space. If looking for an alternative to a traditional bed, consider gracing the head of your bed with a headboard, allowing this element to serve as a focal point in your bedroom.

An iron headboard adds to a bohemian and eclectic vibe in this bedroom.

DESIGN RECIPES TAKEAWAY TIPS

BED SKIRTS

Typically, a headboard is placed against a metal or wood frame since seeing the frame may be undesirable. A bed skirt will help conceal the bed frame. A bed skirt with a sixteen- to eighteen-inch drop typically works best.

UPHOLSTERED HEADBOARDS

To help preserve the longevity of an upholstered headboard, consider having it covered in a stain-resistant or treated fabric, as this will also help to preserve the appearance of your headboard.

To create a custom headboard, opt for batting. A plump and well-wrapped headboard will last longer than one with a thinly wrapped foundation.

METAL HEADBOARDS

Consider an alternative to a traditional headboard, such as iron. Once considered old-fashioned, they are now being used in interior settings for people looking for a mid-century modern or art deco feel.

Toss pillows help to add both texture and color.

PILLOWS

For many interior designers, toss pillows are not only a secret weapon, but also the icing on the cake. Toss pillows, instead of being an afterthought, can and should complete a color story, provide an opportunity to bring in graphics and texture, and serve as a prominent design accessory.

WHERE TO START?

How you arrange pillows can help make or break a room. Whether you like a looser look or one that is more rigid, it is helpful to have a plan. First, sort your pillows by color, then by size. Experiment with different combinations. With beds, it is OK to mix pillows of different textures and patterns.

PILLOW TALK

Some general rules of thumb to keep in mind, for your "top of bed" display: be sure to start from the back and work your way forward. Organize pillows by size, placing the largest pillows in the back and the smallest in the front. A cascading layout in which the heaviest concentration of pillows is in the center and then the display becomes thinner on either end is a traditional option. Another option is to display pillows of the same or similar height and even similar color together.

THROWS

A throw can introduce a new color to a space, blend with existing colors, or act as an accent. For those looking to maintain a more neutral palette, taupe, black, and charcoal gray are some great options. Prefer to incorporate a pop of color? Why not bring into your space warm colors, such as chocolate brown, deep orange, mustard yellow, or rich red?

GUEST BEDROOMS

"GUEST BEDROOMS SHOULD BE USED YEAR-ROUND, NOT AS SHRINES FOR THE OCCASIONAL GUEST."

—Cathy Hobbs

INVITING
SPACES

Soft, soothing colors help to create an inviting guest bedroom.

Guest bedrooms in many homes are discarded spaces. Sometimes they are clutter-filled and cleared just hours before a guest arrives. In other instances, guest bedrooms are left dark and empty, a shrine to the guest who shows up once or twice a year. Guest bedrooms serve as a welcome message to your guests and should be treated as an opportunity to welcome your guests in style.

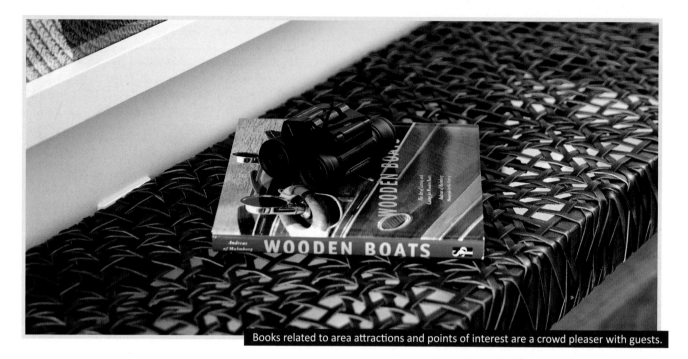

Books related to area attractions and points of interest are a crowd pleaser with guests.

DESIGN RECIPE

WELCOME BASKETS

Welcome baskets are a staple at events such as weddings and large family gatherings—why not create one for your guests? A welcome basket can have the basics such as rolled towels and bottled water or can be enhanced with a specialty item or personalized gift.

BOOKS

Books are a wonderful addition to any guest bedroom. From novels and tourist guides to gorgeous magazines, reading material can be a welcome diversion for your guests.

FRESH FLOWERS

Who doesn't love fresh flowers? Fresh flowers say you took the time to add a special touch to welcome your guest.

TOILETRIES

Sometimes guests forget to bring the basics, such as soap, toothpaste, and even a toothbrush. Having these basics on hand could be a much-appreciated welcome gesture for your guests.

LINENS AND SUCH

For many guests, staying at your home is in lieu of a hotel, so why not make your guest feel like your home is a boutique hotel? Nothing feels better on a bed than sumptuous linens. Extra blankets are also appreciated by guests.

CLASSIC COLORS

Even though it is your home, it is best to stay away from personalized colors. When designing a guest bedroom, it is best to stick with classic colors such as white, blue, yellow, and green. Pastel colors also help to provide a soothing and calming environment.

LOCAL TOUCHES

Coming to your home, in some instances, may be a vacation for your guests. They may even want to learn more about your area and take in some of the local sights and flavors. So why not add some local touches to your guest bedroom? For example, if your area is known for wine, jam, or maple syrup, include these in the welcome basket for your guests.

PROVIDE PRIVACY

Tired and weary, some guests will really welcome the opportunity to have some alone time. Try to create your guest room in an area of the home that provides privacy and, if possible, its own bathroom.

A soft, neutral color palette helps to create a relaxing guest bedroom.

DESIGN RECIPES RULES

CLEAR THE CLUTTER

Ideally, the guest bedroom should not be your catch-all room. Clear the clutter and help make your guest feel like it is their space, even if just for a few days.

CHANGE IT UP

Before it gets old and dusty, keep your guest bedroom fresh and current by changing it up every so often, whether with pillows, artwork, or bedding.

GENDER-NEUTRAL COLORS

Gold and yellow tones are warm and inviting, for a gender-neutral space.

From yellow, blue, gray, and soft pastels, unexpected colors can serve as the perfect color palette for an inviting gender-neutral space. While bright, bold colors can help energize, pale hues can help to create an element of calm.

Gold and mustard not only are gender-neutral but can help enliven a space.

DESIGN RECIPES RULES
WARMER COLORS

YELLOW

Yellow is a great choice especially if you are a fan of gold and brass finishes. Yellow can especially help to perk up or enliven a dark space. Consider both mustard tones as well as pale yellow.

ORANGE

Orange is a happy color that can be seen as both modern and sophisticated. Pairing orange with rich charcoal gray or black can serve as a gorgeous accent color in a bedroom.

PURPLE

Deep purple can feel royal and rich, while softer shades such as lavender not only are gender-neutral but can be bold and attractive, especially when paired with strong, cool colors like charcoal gray. Looking to make an even bolder statement? Pair lavender with black. Conversely, if looking to create a more soothing environment, try pairing lavender with cream or white.

CITRUS COLORS

Citrus colors can include orange, green, and yellow. Citrus colors can really help to brighten and lighten a space, and many shades of colors such as orange and green often have yellow undertones. Citrus colors are also often considered to be gender-neutral and typically hold universal appeal. Citrus colors are also non-trendy, allowing you to enjoy them year-round.

A color palette of blue and gray creates a calm, gender-neutral guest bedroom.

DESIGN RECIPES RULES
COOLER COLORS

BLUE

Blue can be both serene and elegant and can help to create a sense of calm without feeling bland. Blend blue with shades of gray to create a soothing, calm color palette.

GREEN

Green can be a tricky color largely because of how it could be impacted by other colors in a space and even natural light. Deep green tones can feel rich and luxurious, while lighter shades like pastel or mint green can be successful color choices, without appearing medicinal, by pairing them with grounding colors such as gray, brown, and black.

GRAY

From charcoal to soft silver, gray can help create a palette that can also serve as the foundation for your color story.

WARM + COOL
PASTELS

Powder pink, pale blue, soft yellow, and mint green are all colors which used to be associated with youthful rooms and spaces. These days, these colors can be used in modern, décor-forward ways that stand the test of time.

DAYBEDS +
CHAISES
BENCHES +
OTTOMANS

A bench provides a finishing design touch at the foot of a bed.

Daybeds, chaises, benches, and ottomans come in different shapes and sizes, and while some are for actual sleeping, many are not. Often considered as a space-saving alternative to a regular bed, or simply as a space-filler, these versatile furniture pieces can provide a decorative as well as a useful purpose.

A daybed provides a space-saving option in a small guest bedroom.

DESIGN RECIPES RULES

DAYBEDS

Perhaps you picture a daybed as a piece of furniture made of white- or black-painted iron, padded with an ill-fitting mattress, camouflaged with toss pillows. This may have been the standard daybed of decades past, but these days daybeds can serve as an attractive, sleek, and even modern addition to one's home.

STYLES OF DAYBEDS

Daybeds are often long and thin and can come with or without edges or rails. A daybed is wider and bigger than a bench and is often confused with a chaise, which is typically part of a sectional sofa seating grouping. A daybed can be used for extra seating as well as an additional place for sleeping.

CHAISES

Chaises come in different sizes and styles, and work well at the foot of a bed or in a corner. They can be ideal for lounging and relaxation as well as a cozy and space-saving alternative to a small sofa or loveseat.

An oval-shaped bench adds additional seating in this bedroom.

OTTOMANS + BENCHES

Ottomans, typically half the size of a bench, are the most versatile when compared to a daybed or bench. Ottomans can be used either alone or in pairings, often in a set of two or three. Benches, typically longer and more slender than an ottoman, can be used for extra seating, as a footrest, or as a decorative furniture element to introduce a new material or color. Both ottomans and benches come in various shapes including rectangle, circle, square, and oval.

DESIGN RECIPE DOS AND DON'TS

Dos

Do use ottomans and benches when looking for a backless or low-back furniture choice.

Do use ottomans or benches as additional seating.

Do use ottomans and benches to infuse color and texture into a room.

Do use ottomans and benches in areas in which small-scale furniture selections are appropriate.

Do use ottomans and benches to make a design statement.

Don'ts

Don't ignore opportunities to use ottomans and benches as a finishing touch in a space such as at the foot of a bed.

Don't use ottomans and benches in overly large rooms as they may appear too small in large spaces.

Don't use ottomans and benches in ways that don't provide function.

Don't ignore opportunities to use ottomans and benches in unexpected ways such as a table.

Don't forget that ottomans and benches are modular and versatile and can be used in pairs or groupings.

Pink is a color that is both versatile and gender-neutral.

PINK POWER

Fresh and fun, pastel or bold, pink is one of the most versatile and luxurious colors. Pink can be dressed up or dressed down and is also gender-neutral, allowing pink to work well in flexible spaces such as guest bedrooms.

THE FOUNDATIONS OF PINK

Pink comes in different tints, tones, and shades. Many darker pinks have undertones of blue, which is why some of the deeper tones come to life when paired with blue. On the other hand, some pinks, the softer tones, have more cream or white as their foundation color; those work better with lighter shades or can be used as contrast colors when paired with black or brown. Consider using pink as a foundation or springboard for your color story.

QUICK DESIGN RECIPE DOS AND DON'TS

Dos

Do blend tints, tones, and shades of pink to sprinkle hints of color throughout a space.

Do use texture to incorporate pink, such as toss pillows, drapery, throws, and textiles like area rugs.

Do use wall art and wall coverings like wallpaper to introduce pink and pink tones into a room.

Don'ts

Don't add too many different shades of pink in the same room to avoid clashing colors.

Don't overlook opportunities to introduce pink in unexpected ways, such as accessories and florals.

Don't be afraid to use deep shades of pink, such as hot pink and other, richer tones.

A modern Murphy bed conceals a bed ready to be revealed upon a guest's arrival.

DESIGN RECIPES TAKEAWAY TIP

Whether it is for a weekend or longer, there remains a certain protocol when it comes to being a welcomed houseguest. Whether it is an invitation extended by a close friend or business associate, you are going to want to make sure that your stay is pleasant for both you and especially your host and that as a guest, you leave a good impression.

BEING A GOOD GUEST

DON'T ARRIVE EMPTY-HANDED The bottle of wine is perfect to bring to a dinner party, but when it comes to being a houseguest, a more personal gift may do the trick, such as a plant, local guide, or special book.

RESPECT THE HOUSE RULES If everyone is in bed by nine, try not to stay up making noise that may disturb others. Instead, opt to retire to your room and read or watch television in private.

DITCH THE CELLPHONE Someone has invited you into their home and likely wants your attention and time. Nothing is ruder than a guest who is constantly checking emails or making private phone calls.

PARTICIPATE You are there to enjoy your host's company and that of their family. If an invitation is extended to you for an outing, attend, even if the selected activity may not be your preferred pastime.

LEND A HELPING HAND Even if your host seems to have everything under control, offer to help. Even small tasks like making morning coffee or setting the table can be appreciated and help to relieve pressure on your host.

SEND A THANK YOU NOTE Regardless of the length of your stay, be sure to always send a thank you note after your visit.

CHILDREN'S BEDROOMS

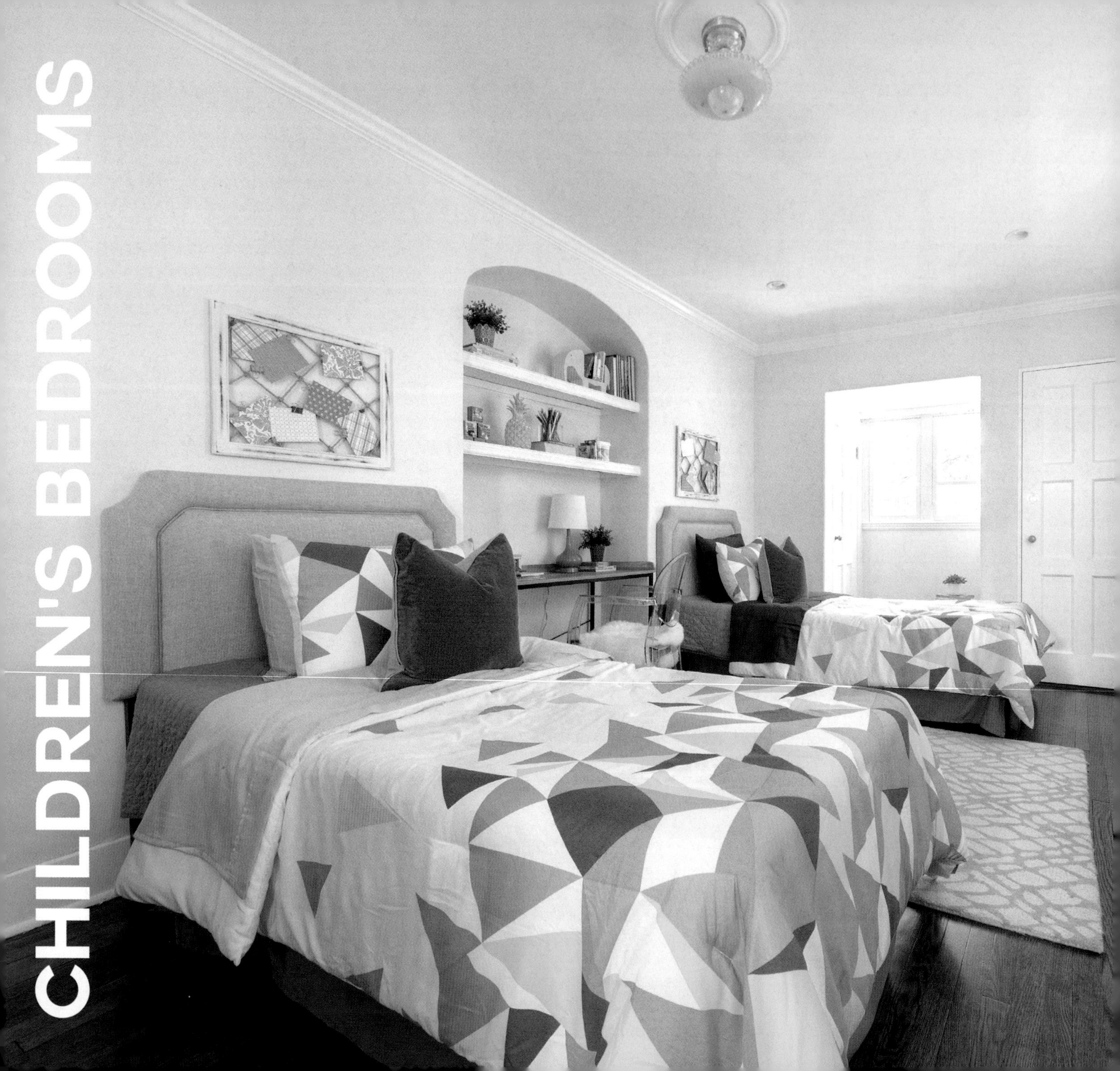

"A CHILD'S BEDROOM SHOULD BE SUN-FILLED, FUN, AND FULL OF VIBRANT AND JOYFUL COLORS."

—Cathy Hobbs

CANDY
COLORS

A child's bedroom designed using cotton candy colors.

Bright, playful, and festive. Candy colors such as yellow, red, orange, blue, and green can add interest and energy while also helping to put a fresh, fun face on a child's bedroom.

A bedroom with striped bedding utilizes fun, candy-colored tones.

Orange is a warm candy color and helps to add energy to children's bedrooms.

DESIGN RECIPE **DOS AND DON'TS**

Dos

Do introduce bright candy colors through accessories and accents such as artwork, bedding, area rugs, and toss pillows.

Do consider adding in a surprise element of color, such as a side chair or ottoman.

Do pair bright, bold colors with neutral colors such as white and black, as neutral colors will help make bright colors stand out.

Don'ts

Don't be afraid to mix various bold colors in a single space.

Don't go overboard. A palette with three to four colors will work well.

Don't pass up opportunities to infuse portable design elements such as a textured toss pillow, fluffy area rug, or plush throw.

A child's bedroom with pale candy colors feels both soothing and fun.

Consider using a candy color for an accent wall.

Use bright, bold candy colors such as hot pink, bright yellow, vibrant green, and ruby red.

Create a color palette that may include a combination of unexpected candy colors.

A simple plaid throw adds a pattern to this child's bedroom.

SPACE-SAVING IDEAS

Built-in beds provide a custom, space-saving alternative to traditional beds.

Children's rooms are often smaller spaces within the home where space is often at a premium. These rooms are also ideal locations for implementing space-saving ideas. From built-ins to shelving and furniture that maximize space, increasing the visual footprint of a child's room is easily achievable by implementing space-saving tips.

Bunk beds are a popular space-saving choice in children's bedrooms.

DESIGN RECIPES TAKEAWAY TIPS

WHERE TO START

Begin by evaluating the need for function within the child's bedroom, the activities that need to happen within the room. Once you have settled on the potential usage, then plan your space, deciding where these activities should take place within the bedroom.

> **ZONES**
>
> Divide a room into distinct zones:
>
> Work • Sleep • Play

ROOM FOR TWO

Shared rooms need to be designed with space in mind. Often there is a need to create mirrored layouts so that space is equally shared, such as an equal number of beds, dressers, desks, and chairs. The configuration of a room dictates flow. Be sure to place key elements in a shared room, like beds, such that entries and exits are clear and unobstructed.

TYPICAL BED CONFIGURATIONS

Two beds separated by single nightstand or side table.
Two beds separated by a desk or worktable.
Two beds separated by a dresser.

Built-ins can provide ideal storage in children's bedrooms.

Custom-made furniture provides the most versatility and flexibility.

BUILT-INS

Built-ins are not always a popular choice in all areas of a home and, when it comes time to renovate, are often the first item a new homeowner may choose to remove. However, when it comes to children's rooms, built-ins such as bookcases and shelving can provide much-needed storage.

DESIGN RECIPES TAKEAWAY TIPS

Decide what you need the built-ins to hold or store.

Consider a mix of closed cabinetry as well as open shelving.

Have a professional measure the area where you are considering adding built-ins.

Select an experienced millworker or company to build and install your built-ins.

Evaluate the ideal design elements for your built-ins such as cabinetry color, finish, and hardware.

WALL STICKERS

Wall stickers provide the opportunity to infuse color and graphics in an easy, affordable, and flexible way.

When it comes to fun, whimsical ideas for a child's bedroom, wallpaper is one of the first ideas that comes to mind. Wallpaper is a great choice to bring color and graphics into a space, while removable wall stickers can infuse creativity and provide more flexibility.

Wall stickers create a focal point in this child's bedroom.

Wall stickers are used to create an instant wall feature.

WHERE TO FIND WALL STICKERS

A host of companies specialize in removable wall stickers. No longer do you have to be limited by size, color, and prints, these days there are plenty of choices. Stores that sell children's bedding, accessories, or wall décor will likely also sell wall stickers. Another unexpected source may be a company that creates large-scale graphics or prints for commercial use. This type of company will be able to produce custom or oversized stickers to create a scene or fill a large wall.

HOW TO BUY

DESIGN RECIPES TAKEAWAY TIPS

Measure both the width and the height of the area you wish to cover with wall stickers.

Check the measurements for the wall stickers to determine how many stickers may be needed. This is critical to avoid having too much or too little.

Allow for mistakes. Be sure to order enough stickers to have extras in case certain stickers need to be adjusted or removed.

Wall stickers serve as the ideal removable alternative to wallpaper.

Black-and-white wall stickers create a graphic element in this bedroom seating area.

PLACING WALL STICKERS

DESIGN RECIPES TAKEAWAY TIPS

Make sure your wall is free of imperfections as these will show once a sticker is put in place.

Allow for some negative or white space. It is not necessary for an entire wall surface to be covered.

Use stickers that allow for easy removal, so that you can adjust as needed.

Place stickers on walls that have a smooth surface. Wall stickers typically do not adhere well to textured surfaces.

Complement your décor. When choosing wall stickers be sure to use stickers that will blend well with the existing colors in your space.

Citrus colors of lemon and lime create a bright, crisp color palette in this child's bedroom.

CITRUS COLORS

From lemons and limes to oranges and grapefruits, the rich and vibrant colors of these juicy fruits can also help to provide bursts of color in your home. Many citrus colors blend well together and in nearly every instance convey a bright, fresh, and cheery message inside the home.

QUICK DESIGN RECIPE

MIX AND MATCH

Mix and match! It is OK to mix various citrus colors in the same room.

USE AS AN ACCENT

Consider using citrus colors as accents. Whether it's an accent pillow and accessory or artwork and area rug, find an easy and affordable way to infuse citrus colors into your home!

COLORS THAT WORK

Pair citrus colors with neutral colors and tones such as white, black, and tan. These colors work well to create a sense of contrast.

COLOR REPETITION

Repeat citrus colors throughout a room or home. Repeating or "mapping" the same or similar colors throughout a space helps to create a space that is both inviting and cohesive.

AFFORDABLE CHILDREN'S ROOM HACKS

When it comes to children's rooms, good design doesn't have to break the bank. After all, beautiful design doesn't have to be expensive to look expensive. As a child grows, their tastes and needs evolve. As a result, designing a child-friendly space should be adaptive and flexible as well as affordable.

BOOKCASES

Bookcases can be used for both aesthetics and functionality. Use them for display as well as storage.

SHELVES

Shelves can provide a functional, space-saving, and affordable way to showcase collectibles and treasured items. Looking for a unique and creative spin on traditional shelving? Try crafting shelves utilizing a unique material or unexpected object.

CHILD-FRIENDLY FURNITURE

Ottomans   Poofs and floor pillows
Benches   Teepees and tents

QUICK DESIGN RECIPES HACK
CREATIVE SHELVING IDEAS

Books   Baseball bats
Industrial piping   Skateboards
Reclaimed wood

A child's bedroom is made unique and fun through the creative use of alternative shelving.

Skateboards are used as shelves.

195

LOWER LEVELS + BASEMENTS

"A HOME SHOULDN'T STOP AT THE STAIRWELL TO THE BASEMENT. AN ENTIRE HOME SHOULD BE USED."

—Cathy Hobbs

BUILT-INS

Built-ins are used for both books and collectibles.

Built-ins remain popular in interior design, even though they do have their positives and negatives. In the positive column are the space-saving benefits, while the negative column is dominated by the perception that built-ins create a dated look. What are the best ways to incorporate built-ins into your home? Many designers believe the best rule of thumb is to "think function first," ensuring you have a clear purpose when looking to bring the beauty of built-ins into your home.

A built-in holds a menagerie of accessories.

DESIGN RECIPE DOS AND DON'TS

Dos

Do utilize materials for your built-ins that will blend with the overall feel and architectural bones of your home.

Do paint built-ins the same color as your walls for a uniform look or contrasting color to add interest.

Do blend a combination of cabinetry to conceal items, while including open shelves to display books and accessories.

Do enlist a custom millworker or craftsman to build your built-ins.

Do make sure that your built-ins have a clear function and purpose.

Don'ts

Don't automatically rip out built-ins that may have a useful purpose and functionality.

Don't purchase pre-made built-ins when possible. Custom-made and measured built-ins are preferred.

Don't use materials that could become easily damaged, discolored, or rusted. Solid wood is often the preferred material.

Don't overlook affordable options to create the look of built-ins, such as using pre-built cabinetry.

Don't ignore ways to help make built-ins shine by using interesting materials and finishes for elements such as countertops and handles.

Custom built-in millwork showcases both open shelves and closed cabinetry.

QUICK DESIGN RECIPE

SHELVES

WHAT TO DISPLAY

Framed photography • Treasured mementos
Greenery • Accessories and accents • Books

BLACK + WHITE

Black or white shelving, depending on your wall color, can provide a bold sense of contrast while also adding an interesting design element. Additionally, blending a combination of black and white accessories or incorporating black-and-white photography can infuse a modern, yet minimalist vibe.

FAMILY SPACES

A family space incorporates bright, friendly colors.

Basements and the lower levels of a home are popular locations to create family-friendly spaces. These spaces are typically large, spacious, and open, but can pose a challenge for homeowners when it comes to function, feel, and design.

A family room is divided into a lounge zone and an entertainment zone.

QUICK DESIGN RECIPE

FAMILY-FRIENDLY DESIGN TIP

Because basements and lower levels are often large, consider dividing a space into zones to maximize space and function.

FAMILY-FRIENDLY ZONES

ENTERTAINMENT ZONE

An entertainment zone can serve as a space for playing games and movie-watching.

LOUNGE ZONE

A lounge zone can be a space for entertaining and for activities like reading and lounging.

WORK ZONE

A work zone can be more of an adult space for work or related activities, or it can be where homework takes place.

Certain colors, like gray, help to hide stains in family-friendly spaces.

FAMILY-FRIENDLY MATERIALS

The ideal family-friendly materials are easy to wipe, wash, or clean.

MATERIALS

Leather • Leather alternatives, like vegan leather • Hospitality- + commercial-grade fabrics

FAMILY-FRIENDLY COLORS

Orange • Red • Yellow • Green

STAIN-RESISTANT COLORS

Gray • Black • Brown • Blue

DESIGN RECIPES TAKEAWAY TIP

Since lower levels and basements typically don't receive an abundance of light, choose bright, friendly colors to make a space feel lighter. Also make sure to incorporate lots of lighting, such as overhead lighting, table lamps, and floor lamps.

BIG ART

A large piece of art helps to serve as a focal point in this family room.

Whether your home is large or small, artwork in many instances can make or break a room. In design, artwork is often seen as the "icing on the cake." Big or large-scale art can instantly help to create a focal point or make a bold design statement. Big art can also work wonders, especially in rooms with high ceilings.

Identically pieces of art can be hung side-by-side or on top of each other to create a large, single, cohesive work of art.

DESIGN RECIPE DOS AND DON'TS

Dos

Do use identical or similar artwork in a series. This is one of the best ways to create a diptych (two pieces of art in a series) or a triptych (three pieces).

Do consider using a group of smaller art pieces or mirrors to fill a space or wall.

Do hang artwork both vertically and horizontally to make a big art statement. Similar or identical artwork can feel like a single art piece when hung side-by-side or one on top of the other.

Don'ts

Don't be afraid to experiment with color. While neutral colors such as black and white can be impactful, so can a bold use of color.

Don't overlook artwork alternatives such as mirrors. Mirrors placed in a series can make a bold and impactful statement.

Don't hang large artwork too close to the ceiling. In general, many people hang their artwork too low or too high. A general rule of thumb is to hang artwork so that the center point is at five feet.

A harmonious combination of artwork, shelving, and mirrors is used as a wall solution in this lounge space.

WALL SOLUTIONS

When it comes to artwork, sometimes thinking outside the box can be the best solution. Gone are the days of solely using traditional prints or painted canvases; in are the days of creativity, including innovative elements to add interest and sparkle to your walls.

DESIGN RECIPES TAKEAWAY TIPS

Paint an accent wall. There are so many ways to perk up a space using paint.

Include wall hangings or elements in place of traditional artwork.

Incorporate black-and-white photography.

Consider substituting shelving for artwork.

Frame children's artwork or use shadow boxes.

Look for colorful elements to frame, such as scarves or large pieces of fabric.

A leaning mirror provides a wall accent in a space with exposed brick walls.

BRICK + PANELED WALLS

In older homes especially, paneled walls are common, as this was once a popular architectural feature, particularly in lower levels and basements. While exposed brick, typically found in industrial and even historical spaces, has high appeal, both architecture features have their design challenges. Often it is difficult to hang artwork or mirrors on brick or paneled walls; additionally, these architectural features may limit or restrict furniture layout.

DESIGN RECIPES TAKEAWAY TIPS

EMBRACE IT

Don't try to cover up or conceal. While covering brick or paneled walls with drywall is an option, consider allowing this unique feature to shine!

LEAN IT

Look for ways to highlight exposed brick or paneled walls using non-hangable wall pieces such as leaning mirrors or oversized artwork that can also be leaned.

DRILL IT

Use a masonry drill to hang a piece of art, cabinet, or wall hanging. You can often drill between bricks.

PAINT IT

For many, painting over paneled or exposed brick walls is a way to infuse a modern, clean, updated look.

WALLPAPER IT

Use wallpaper to add interest to a space.

A home gym is a popular design option for a lower level space.

FINISHED BASEMENTS

Dungeons, caves, no man's lands, these are just some of the words and descriptors that may come to mind when referring to the basement level of a home. Use every space in your home as opposed to having what, in many cases, is a large, underutilized area. In many parts of the country, having a home with a finished basement is a desirable selling feature. In other areas, where space may be at a premium, ensuring a basement is fully functional and utilized to the fullest may be an absolute must.

DESIGN SOLUTIONS

Typically, basements are generous in size, often the length and width of the entire home.

FINISHED BASEMENT DESIGN OPTIONS

Playrooms	Home offices
Home theaters	Home gyms
Spas	Family rooms

DESIGN RECIPES TAKEAWAY TIPS

Add plenty of soft surfaces, such as wall-to-wall carpeting or oversized area rugs.

Mix fabric and leather furniture pieces. Leather is a durable choice, as are hospitality- or commercial-grade fabrics. These fabrics are long-lasting and come in a variety of textures and colors.

Add a dehumidifier. Basements often retain moisture. A dehumidifier will reduce moisture and improve air quality.

Let there be light! Lighting can truly go a long way in making a basement space feel bright and cheery.

Select light rather than dark colors for your furniture and accents. Instead of dark and gloomy, opt for a light and bright color palette.

BONUS RECIPES

"HOME DESIGN RECIPES GOES BEYOND ROOM-BY-ROOM GUIDES, TRANSLATING TO EVERYDAY LIVING."

—Cathy Hobbs

HOME STAGING

"MOST BUYERS LACK VISION; HOME STAGING IS A CRITICAL MARKETING TOOL TO HELP SELL ANY PROPERTY."

—Cathy Hobbs

STAGING + STYLING

Accents and accessories are key design elements in home staging.

STAGE IT. SELL IT!

You only have one chance to make a first impression. If a potential buyer doesn't like what they see on the first viewing, it is unlikely that same buyer will return even with the lure of knowledge that the residence has been renovated, updated, or staged.

Today's buyers not only have bargaining power but their choice of properties, which makes them a savvy and often picky bunch. Home sellers must have similar savviness if they wish to sell their properties for top dollar in the shortest amount of time. How a home is staged is the key to this success.

The beauty of home staging is that it does not have to cost a lot of money to achieve a jaw-dropping transformation. The first step is to have a professional home stager, real estate agent, or friend walk through the property objectively, pointing out potential negatives that could sink a sale or downgrade an offer. If they notice something negative, potential buyers will too!

Living room before staging.

Living room after staging.

DESIGN RECIPES RULES

When a seller puts their property on the market it is no longer their home, but a product on the market for sale, like an item on a grocery store shelf. For that property to attract the greatest number of potential buyers, it must be portrayed in the best possible light. Properties that are worn, tired, and—worst of all—cluttered simply do not show well. Most potential buyers are not looking for worry and work, but properties that are "move-in ready." Properties that present as a project, often referred to as "handyman specials," will be forced to adjust price tags to reflect their shortcomings.

Don't forget to begin your home staging journey with curb appeal, staging both the exterior and interior of your home. Many potential buyers won't even exit their vehicles or come through the front door to view a property if they are turned off by a home's exterior.

DESIGN RECIPES TAKEAWAY TIPS

Neutralize

Declutter

Depersonalize

Minimize to maximize space

Invest in minor repairs

DESIGN RECIPE

WHAT IS STAGING?

Staging, in basic terms, is the preparation of a home for sale so that it appeals to the largest number of potential buyers and sells for the most amount of money in the shortest amount of time.

GETTING STARTED

Start with foundation pieces and end with the small details. In other words, start big and end small. Begin with large items like sofas and area rugs, then focus on complementary elements like artwork, and end with details such as toss pillows, throws, and accessories.

ROOMS TO STAGE

Living rooms and master bedrooms are, in nearly all cases, two of the most important rooms in a home. Key areas to stage are the entry, living room, dining room, and master bedroom suite.

FURNITURE ARRANGING

The goal in staging is to create a cohesive furniture arrangement. In home selling, less is more. The goal is to allow potential buyers to be able to see the space, as opposed to focusing on the stuff, so when in doubt, take it out.

STAGING-FRIENDLY COLORS

Neutral color palettes are ideal for staging. Neutral colors blend with other colors, while also creating a soothing environment that will create move-in ready appeal. Staging-friendly colors include off-white, taupe, gray, brown, and black.

Living room before staging.

Living room after staging.

PHOTOGRAPHY

HDMI - 1080i59.94   12:53 PM   BAT1:

A well-photographed interior is about capturing the perfect angle.

LIGHTS. CAMERA. ACTION!

When it comes time to sell your home, photos may make all the difference. The reality is nearly all potential buyers spend time perusing photographs online before deciding if they wish to see a property in person. This is where the power of photography comes into play. With the invention of lower-priced, high-quality cameras and even cell phones, it is possible for homeowners to take good-quality photographs on their own. Still, others may choose to leave the job to a professional. Regardless, there are some photography tips one should keep in mind to make sure a property is ready for its close-up!

A living room captured by a nonprofessional photographer.

TOP TEN TIPS

1. Pay attention to the sun. Sun can make a difference, especially in a space that may not get a lot of daylight. Even lighting conditions and sunny days are best.

2. Use natural light as much as possible.

3. Consider hiring a professional. Working with a professional photographer doesn't have to break the bank. Great photography can do wonders for properly showcasing a home.

4. Look for interesting angles and vignettes. Creative angles can help to inspire interest, while vignettes work well to highlight unique design elements or décor.

5. Highlight special or unique architectural features.

6. Avoid, if possible, shooting toward windows or glass doors. Light can spill into a room, creating a washed-out effect.

7. Choose a sunny day. Cloudy or rainy days will require considerable additional light that could make photographs look artificial.

8. Add pops of color to a neutral space to add a sense of contrast.

9. Turn lights off. This common technique used by professional photographers allows for the best flexibility for color and light corrections in postproduction.

10. Use reflective surfaces like mirrors to help bounce light in a room, which will help to create a feeling of spaciousness.

The same living room staged and photographed by a professional photographer.

QUICK DESIGN RECIPE **DOS AND DON'TS**

Dos

Do take photographs either in the late morning or early afternoon; this is typically when lighting is optimal. Never take photographs at night.

Do keep the lights off! If lights are turned on, it is very difficult to adjust lighting in postproduction.

Do tell a story. Whether you choose to hire a professional stager or style the space yourself, tell a story using similar colors, finishes, or complementary décor.

Don'ts

Don't forget areas like kitchens and bathrooms. These areas are important for home selling.

Don't overstuff a room. A photograph can make a space feel smaller than it is in person; if in doubt, edit.

Don't use the flash. Unless you are a professional, using flash may create unwanted shadows. Instead, opt for a manual setting on a professional digital camera.

A living room photographed for the purpose of home selling.

A unique angle captures an architectural feature of the same living space.

A photograph captures the overall décor and feel of this living room.

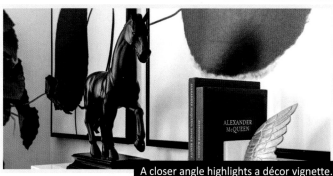

A closer angle highlights a décor vignette.

Lifestyle elements as displayed in a staged kitchen.

FAVE TIPS

SET THE MOOD

Determine the mood you want to create or message you want to send within a space and then incorporate the appropriate lifestyle elements. For example, to create a message of a spa-like bathroom, lifestyle elements could include candles or bath salts.

DETERMINE A COLOR SCHEME

The ideal color scheme typically consists of three colors.

WHO WILL BUY THIS HOUSE?

Consider the end user. The foundation of lifestyle selling is to appeal to the potential buyer, considering how they will likely wish to live and function in the home.

LOOK LIKE A MODEL

Create the look of a model home. Staging is neutralizing and depersonalizing as well as adding lifestyle elements that give the feeling of a space that is lived in. Don't ignore areas such as kitchens and closets. Many potential buyers find elements like organized, generous storage options to be a bonus.

Simple refreshments like still or sparkling water and a few nibbles are sufficient to provide at an open house.

DESIGN RECIPE

CREATE AN ATMOSPHERE

First and foremost, an open house is an opportunity to entertain and educate, and like any other event that one may host in their home, an open house is a chance for the home seller to showcase their home by highlighting the positives and downplaying the negatives.

FIRST IMPRESSIONS

At the open house, it is important for a home seller to create a "moment" the second a potential buyer walks in the door. The reality is that most buyers decide about a property within the first three minutes, whether positive or negative, so it is critical that the first impression is strong.

ENTRY DÉCOR

DESIGN RECIPES TAKEAWAY TIPS: FIRST IMPRESSIONS

A vase of fresh flowers upon entry. From a single stem to a handful of flowers, florals instantly say "welcome" to potential buyers.

Beyond the traditional real estate agent property brochure, consider infusing a unique and crafty touch. Try making crafted cork coasters using a photo of the home or floor plan of a key room, and place them on an entry console.

A small bowl of fruit or vegetables on a kitchen counter or island. Fruits and vegetables not only are affordable but add color. Options include artichokes, peppers, apples, lemons, or limes.

VACATION HOMES

"THE MAGICAL EXPERIENCE OF A VACATION HOME COMES TO LIFE THROUGH A COMBINATION OF PLANNING AND DESIGN."

—Cathy Hobbs

SEASIDE DÉCOR

Nautical-inspired elements fill the living room of this vacation home.

Relaxed and easy, soft and light, these are some of the design aesthetics that often come to mind when one thinks of seaside décor. While bright colors can infuse a space with interest and excitement, soothing tones and materials can help to create a design that is tranquil and timeless without attempting to compete with the beauty of a seaside environment.

Soft, neutral fabrics are paired with blue accents in this master bedroom.

Wood elements help to infuse organic elements into the living room of this vacation home.

DESIGN RECIPES TAKEAWAY TIPS

INSPIRATION

Use the architecture and environment surrounding the home as your guide. Through design, look for ways to enhance the existing bones of your space as opposed to competing with it. Be inspired by surrounding elements such as the color of water or foliage.

COLOR

Embrace the colors of your surrounding environment, whether it is the color of sand, water, a boat dock, or elements in nature like native landscaping. As you design your space, try to bring outdoor colors and hues into your space. Consider blues or greens as accent colors. These colors work especially well with a neutral color palette and colors such as white and taupe and will play well with a seaside design vibe.

NATURE

Look for ways to bring the outside in. Be inspired to bring some of the outdoor elements around you into your indoor environment. This can mean anything from infusing wood into a space to elements like sand and stone.

LIGHT + BRIGHT

Stay light and bright. Creating a neutral palette is ideal for a seaside designed space. This helps to create a base or foundation for the rest of your color palette.

Boat oars hang as artwork in a nautical-inspired vacation home.

Nature-inspired elements help to infuse a space with a sense of the outdoors.

QUICK DESIGN RECIPE

SEASIDE DÉCOR TIPS

Paddles and oars

Sailcloth fabric

Rattan and woven rope

Sand and stone

Water or nautical-inspired artwork

Wood elements

Light, neutral fabrics

MODERN
COUNTRY

A blend of wood elements and cotton fabrics provides a modern, yet rustic vibe.

From slipcovers to painted floors and reclaimed wood, myriad design elements are typically considered to be country-inspired décor. Add a twist, by combining modern furnishings with industrial and even rustic finds to create a modern country design style.

QUICK DESIGN RECIPE

VINTAGE + SALVAGE

Reclaimed, recycled, and salvaged items are a creative way to infuse an interesting and one-of-a-kind element into nearly any room of the home. Beyond furniture and accessories, consider specialty elements or antiques, such as stained-glass windows, old doors, textiles, or vintage doorknobs.

POTTERY + JARS

Pottery provides a colorful, artisan element while also serving a purpose depending on its style. While jars are useful in numerous ways, crafty ideas include painting mason jars muted colors; they can be rubbed to appear old. You can also wrap portions of the jar with twine or fill with moss and top with a succulent or bloom, using the mason jar as a vase.

DRIED FLOWERS + HERBS

While flowers are one option for those looking for country-inspired décor, other ideas include hanging dried herbs or lavender. The look is organic and attractive as well as fragrant and long-lasting.

SUCCULENTS

Succulents are not only hardy but versatile. Try placing succulents on a small bed of stones or embedded in moss for a modern look. Succulents look especially attractive when paired with natural elements such as wood and branches.

234

Locally owned shops can be a treasure trove of unique finds.

A country store displays the work of local craftspeople and artisans.

Antique stores are a great option for reclaimed and salvaged goods.

DESIGN RECIPES RULES

BUYING SALVAGE

Salvage yards, flea markets, and local consignment stores are often a treasure trove of fabulous finds, from old doors to furniture, kitchen cabinets, and more.

TOP TIPS

GO ONLINE

In many instances, vendors will have photographs of their inventory online. While many will not allow you to place items on hold, having a preselection of items on your wish list will help to maximize your trip.

COMPARISON SHOP

Avoid love at first sight. In many instances, more than one vendor will sell the same or similar items, allowing you to comparison shop. While most vendors will accept credit cards, be sure to bring plenty of cash, as it will be nearly impossible to have any bargaining power without it.

TAKE A FIELD TRIP

Even if you love what you see online, it is ideal to view your selections in person. When possible, take the time to visit a local vendor, store, or market.

Vacation homes can be a blend of soothing yet durable furnishings.

GETTING STARTED

The first aspect to consider when furnishing your weekend or vacation home is how the home will be used. Will it be used solely for your family to enjoy, or will it be rented out and used partially as an investment property? Keep in mind, a home used for rental purposes will receive more wear and tear than one used just for your own personal use, thus requiring an increased focus on budget-friendly, yet highly durable design selections.

SOFAS

An investment in a good-quality sofa should top your list. Choose a sofa made of kiln-dried hardwood as opposed to a softwood such as pine. Feel the back of the sofa and, if possible, view underneath its frame. You should not feel or see staples, nails, or wood; these are indications of a poorly wrapped frame. For longevity, choose sofa cushions that are partial down or foam-filled, as opposed to those filled with pure down. Select commercial- or hospitality-grade fabrics as they are both stain-resistant and intended for heavy use.

FLOORING

Flooring for an investment property should be durable, so be sure to select a low-maintenance flooring solution such as porcelain tile, laminate, or hardwood that is well sealed.

COLORS
STAIN-RESISTANT COLORS

Gray

Blue

Brown

Black

TOP TEN TIPS

1. Design for your target audience. Remember you are marketing an experience.

2. Provide a welcome basket with items such as area maps, bottled water, snacks, local wine, honey, or maple syrup.

3. Purchase a sleeper sofa. The more people the property can sleep, the higher the rental fee.

4. Consider hiring a professional staging company. Staging companies specialize in setting a space.

5. Pay for professional photography. Potential renters often decide about a property based on photography and design.

6. Don't deceive or conceal. Renters will expect and demand the property they viewed in your photographs.

7. Make sure your property is spick-and-span clean.

8. Design using a blend of pieces that are "high and low." Good design doesn't have to be expensive to look expensive.

9. Splurge on items that touch the skin, such as towels and bedding. Also include extra sets of sheets and blankets.

10. Create a neutral and appealing décor; many people are turned off by personal colors and décor items.

SHORT-TERM RENTAL DESIGN

From beach locations to suburban environments, short-term rentals are an attractive alternative to traditional hotels, especially for families. While renting your home as-is may save on costs, showing a property at its very best will lead to better photos and ultimately more bookings.

Many renters will want to bring a four-legged friend.

PET + CHILD-FRIENDLY DESIGN TIPS

Washable and wipeable fabrics

Cushions with removable covers for easy washing or replacement

Leather and faux leather

Sturdy construction

THINGS TO AVOID

Bouclé or woven/knit fabrics

Velvet or materials that will easily show dirt or pet hair

Glass or items that can easily chip, break, or potentially cause injuries

"NEUTRAL COLORS ARE THE IDEAL FOUNDATION FOR A COLOR STORY THAT IS THEN SPRINKLED WITH 'POPS' OF COLOR."

—Cathy Hobbs

BLACK +
WHITE

Off-white upholstery is paired with black-and-white accents.

To create the perfect color palette, nothing is quite as pure, timeless, and versatile as decorating using black-and-white. Black-and-white simply serves as the perfect blank slate for creating virtually any color scheme you desire. An all-white color palette can be crisp and fresh. Conversely, a pure-black palette can add a sense of luxury and elegance. The combination of the two—a color palette using both black-and-white—can be the foundation for a simply stunning interior.

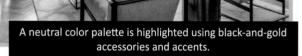

A neutral color palette is highlighted using black-and-gold accessories and accents.

Black-and-white artwork and accessories make this bedroom neutral, yet impactful.

DESIGN RECIPE DOS AND DON'TS

Dos

Do leave negative space in a room. In many instances, leaving soffits, certain walls, moldings, and trims white can serve as the perfect accent.

Do blend different tints, tones, and shades in a room. It is OK to blend ivory and cream with pure white.

Do incorporate black-and-white into a space with the help of portable accessories such as toss pillows, throws, and coffee-table books.

Do consider an all black-and-white color scheme. Black-and-white is truly a luxurious color combination and can be enhanced further if desired by adding accent finishes such as brass, nickel, or chrome.

Do purchase neutral upholstered furniture pieces like sofas and chairs in either black or white. These pieces will be versatile and easily incorporated into existing décor.

Don'ts

Don't ignore the opportunity to create a black-and-white color palette in small areas like bathrooms.

Don't use different shades of black. Unlike white, different shades of black may look "dusty" in a space.

Don't blend too many additional colors with a black-and-white color palette, which serves as a true foundational palette and is best accented with a single color when possible.

Don't dismiss the power of black-and-white artwork and accessories in a room or space.

Don't use black-and-white colors as throwaways, instead use these colors purposefully. When possible, use techniques called color blocking and color mapping, in which a color is grouped, or "blocked," then repeated, or "mapped," throughout a space to create a cohesive look.

Various black-and-white design elements are repeated and used to create a bold, black-and-white space.

DESIGN RECIPES RULES

SIX WAYS TO INCORPORATE BLACK-AND-WHITE

CHOOSE A DESIGN STYLE

Decide on your design style. Modern, transitional, contemporary, or traditional, for example. Choosing a design style will serve as the foundation for your design plan and help in selecting furniture and accessory pieces for your décor.

PAINT AN ACCENT WALL

Using an accent wall can be the perfect way to introduce a bold element like black into your décor.

SELECT A SIGNATURE PIECE

A signature piece can be an area rug with a big, bold graphic pattern or a fabulous piece of artwork or gorgeous chandelier. Whatever piece you select will serve as the anchor for the room and help you to fill in the rest of your design.

BUY LARGE THEN SMALL

Purchase large pieces first, then accessorize. Once you have selected the signature piece that you feel best represents your personal taste and style, allow it to serve as your inspiration. After this, choose your largest pieces first, then your smaller pieces like accents and accessories.

USE TINTS, TONES, AND SHADES

Various tones and tints of white can be an interesting design choice, as well as different shades of almost-black, like dark gray. While different shades of black may appear "dusty," different shades of gray such as charcoal can work well when sprinkled throughout your space.

ADD POPS OF COLOR

One of the most versatile design aspects of working with black and white is the fact that they are foundation colors that help to create a neutral canvas. Virtually any color can pop when placed against black or white. When using black or white, or a combination of the two, consider adding a pop of color to liven up your space.

COLOR BLOCKING AND MAPPING

Shades of pink are grouped, or "blocked," and repeated, or "mapped," throughout this living space.

CREATING A COLOR SCHEME

Have you ever looked at a space and wondered what makes it so inviting? Why do the colors just work? Color is one of those design tools that can often make or break a space. Choose the wrong colors and a room feels disjointed. Choose the right colors and the same space comes to life and feels cohesive.

Designer techniques called color blocking and color mapping are two tricks of the trade in which a color is grouped (or "blocked"), and then repeated (or "mapped") throughout a space. These techniques, if used effectively, can help to create a space that is colorful without being overwhelming.

Two prominent colors, turquoise and orange, are color blocked and then color mapped in this living space.

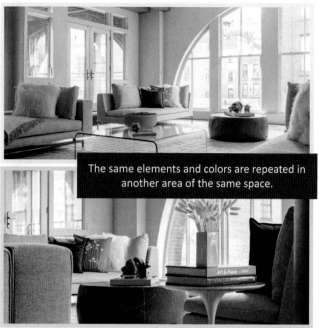

The same elements and colors are repeated in another area of the same space.

DESIGN RECIPE **DOS AND DON'TS**

Dos

Do begin by choosing the colors with which to create your color palette. Typically, selecting two to three colors is best.

Do incorporate other elements in the space that display the individual colors selected for your color palette, such as artwork, area rugs, accessories, accents, and even books.

Do group/block and repeat/map your color palette colors, sprinkling them throughout a room.

Do use color blocking and color mapping techniques to connect color within different areas of the same room or different rooms in a home.

Do repeat finishes within a space such as gold or chrome.

Don'ts

Don't choose colors that are all the same shade. It is, however, acceptable to choose different tints, tones, and shades of the same color.

Don't forget to incorporate negative color space in a room. Leaving open color opportunities will help the colors that are present to shine.

Don't avoid colors such as black and white. These colors not only help to create an elegant sense of contrast but are also great foundation colors for modern design.

Don't use more than three colors to color block or color map.

Don't ignore the influence lighting may have on color. Colors can change appearance based on their location within a home and time of day.

A color palette of black, white, and powder pink is repeated within this bedroom.

DESIGN RECIPES CHECKLIST

DESIGN RECIPES COLOR BLOCKING AND COLOR MAPPING MUST-HAVES

✓ Pick a color or colors to serve as the foundation for your color story.

✓ Repeat the color or colors in various ways throughout the space.

✓ Create interesting opportunities to repeat color through artwork, upholstery, accessories, accents, and more.

The dominant color, yellow, is repeated in various ways in this bedroom.

QUICK DESIGN HACK

Never have a prominent color stand alone. If you introduce a color into a space, repeat the color elsewhere in the same room. Also, be careful not to have different color themes throughout your home. Instead, use color as a connector, picking up a color or pair of colors in a space and then purposefully, yet sparingly, weave those colors throughout your home.

A small office painted in Benjamin Moore Color 126, Pumpkin Spice.

NAVIGATING THE PAINT AISLE

In nearly all home-improvement stores, the paint aisles are divided by brand and type, as far as interior versus exterior paints. Exterior paints are specifically formulated to withstand the elements and are more durable than paints intended solely for interior use. Many brands offer paints suitable for both indoor and outdoor paint applications.

WHAT'S IN A NAME?

Once you have selected the type of paint you are looking for, to help narrow down your selection, next, select a brand. The best advice is to do your research and read reviews. One of the biggest differentiators is price. There can often be a substantial price difference between different brands of paint. A higher price tag does not always mean higher quality. You can often get superb quality paint as far as coverage and durability with a paint that is sold at a lower price point.

COLOR

Most professional paint stores can easily match colors. Often this can be achieved using even small color samples.

FINISH

Selecting a finish will likely be your final step. In general, the higher the paint gloss the easier it is to clean. However, if you have brand-new walls, a flat or matte finish may be your best choice to create a beautiful, smooth finish.

TYPES OF PAINT FINISHES

Flat	Satin
Matte	Semi-Gloss
Eggshell	High Gloss
Pearl	

CHOOSING A PAINT COLOR

Perhaps you have stood in the paint aisle staring at all the little paint chips on display, with confusion and even fear relating to what to do next? Well, you are not alone. For many homeowners, choosing interior paint colors is one of the biggest and most controversial decisions relating to their home purchase.

A living room with a monochromatic color scheme using tints, tones, and shades of cream.

A monochromatic color scheme with hints of mushroom and gray.

MONOCHROMATIC COLOR SCHEMES

Monochromatic (or tone-on-tone) color schemes can be luxurious and elegant while also serving as the perfect foundation for pops of color, metallic accents, and a strong sense of contrast.

CREATING A MONOCHROMATIC COLOR SCHEME

Begin with a neutral color to serve as the foundation for your monochromatic color palette. Popular choices include white, gray, and brown. Foundational colors allow for a base with which to build a color palette or color story. After selecting a color for your monochromatic color scheme, utilize tints, tones, and shades of that color to create a color palette.

WHY WHITE

White isn't just a single shade. From cool to warm, there are myriad shades of white. White serves as one of the most versatile color choices to create a monochromatic color scheme, as it allows one to blend tints, tones, and shades as well as integrate pops of color. Use mirrors in white-on-white color schemes to bounce light.

GRAY AND TAUPE

Infuse cool gray and deep taupe in spaces that have an abundance of light or a space you wish to cool down. Conversely, use warm gray and brown tones in spaces that you wish to feel cozy.

ADDING COLOR

Pops of color can help enliven and uplift a monochromatic color scheme, while also allowing for versatility. Bring in bold, deep, rich colors to add a sense of contrast. Consider pastels to blend soft color into a neutral color palette. Metallic finishes, materials like stone, and textiles such as area rugs, toss pillows, and throws can also serve as design tools to help integrate color.

FINAL THOUGHTS

ACKNOWLEDGMENTS + THANK YOUS

I begin by saying that I did not get here by myself. The journey, albeit rewarding, was a long one. I want to first thank my parents, who never made me EVER believe that I couldn't accomplish something if I set my mind to it. They instilled in me a doctrine to always do my best and to finish what I start. This allowed me, in the end, to take an unexpected career path, first as a TV news reporter, followed by a second act as an interior designer.

Flashback to my senior year in college, and a milestone (then called "Meet the Firms Day"). EVERY senior attended; this was the day dozens of companies interviewed soon-to-be graduates, often handing out job offers on the spot. I remember calling my father and telling him I wasn't going to attend. "But why?" he asked. "Because I want to be a television news reporter, and, if I go, I am going to get a job and be sidetracked from my career goal," I explained. "What are you going to do for money?" my father bristled. "I have it all figured out; I just got a job as a valet. I am going to park cars until I get my first TV job," I said. There was a BIG pause on the other end of the phone. Then came a series of magical words that guide me to this day. "Cathy, I believe in you," my dad said. Those incredible words were all I needed to hear. I stayed home on "Meet the Firms Day" and worked as a valet

until I landed my first reporting job six months later. My father sadly died at fifty, just as I started my career.

My incredible mother has been a profound inspiration to me, encouraging me every step of the way. I cannot thank her enough for her love and support. My biggest "cheerleader," my husband, is the reason I am an interior designer. When I decided to attend interior design school while still working as a television news reporter, my husband supported me in every way one can be supported by a partner, believing in me and encouraging me, to the point of literally helping me with homework assignments! Now that's love. In the decades since, he has listened to my ideas and plans for my interior design business and provided unlimited support for my dreams and goals. He is the rock of our family. I want to thank him for walking next to me on my life's journey.

To my dedicated, loyal, and unbelievably talented team at my design company, Cathy Hobbs Design Recipes. The gorgeous, curated designs we produce make me so proud and are the foundation for the recipes that fill the pages of *Home Design Recipes*. Thank you to our long-time photographer, Scott G. Morris of SGM Photography, a true artist.

To the team at Mango, you loved the idea for this book from the start. I want to thank my publisher, Brenda Knight, who fought for and championed this book every step of the way. You are truly amazing! Hugs to managing editor Robin Miller. And gratitude to CEO Christopher McKenney for pressing forward despite initial bumps in the road.

Lastly, a huge thank you to so many friends who provided support for me and *Home Design Recipes*. A major shout-out to Roy Fenichel, my copy editor to the rescue. A special thank you to Nigel for capturing me in my "best light" for my author photo, and for his beautiful foreword. And immense gratitude to Thom, Ryan, Laila, Barbara, Amir, Tamron, Shell, Robert, Jason, Joseph, Tyler, Kyan, Michael, Evette, Kim, Dottie, Michele, Tamsen, George, Stephen, and Paula, whose introduction to the team at Mango helped to make the publishing of this book possible.

On one of many vacations with Mama

My favorite photo of Daddy and Me

CREDITS

PHOTOGRAPHY CREDITS

Hobbs, Cathy—pages 20-24, 26-27, 29, 31-33, 46-47, 64, 145 (right image), 188, 208, 232, 234-235, 237, 248, and page 253.

Morris, Scott G. (SGM Photography)—pages 2-3, 5, 11-12, 18, 25, 28, 30, 34, 36-45, 48-50, 52-63, 65-66, 68-82, 84-100, 102-116, 118-132, 134-144, 145 (left image), 146-148, 150-164, 166-180, 182-187, 189-196, 198-207, 209-212, 214, 216-217, 218 (bottom image), 219 (bottom image), 221, 222 (bottom image), 223-226, 228-231, 236, 238, 240-247, and page 249.

Cathy Hobbs Design Recipes—pages 20-24, 26-27, 29, 31-33, 46-47, 64, 145 (right image), 188, 208, 218 (top image), 219 (top image), 220, 222 (top image), 232-235, 237, 248, and page 253.

SPECIAL IMAGE CREDITS

Omura, Sarah—pages 1, 259, and page 260.

BACK OF BOOK IMAGE CREDITS

Barker, Nigel—page 256

Morris, Scott G. (SGM Photography)—pages 250-251 and page 254.

ABOUT THE AUTHOR

Cathy Hobbs, ASID, LEED AP, is a five-time Emmy award-winning former television news reporter turned interior designer, home stager, and nationally syndicated design writer. Cathy is a tour de force and prolifically creative dynamo in the fields of interior design, real estate staging, and home selling. Cathy's broad range of curated ideas for the home has captured the national attention of homeowners, real estate agents, and design enthusiasts. Her practical, easy-to-follow design techniques have led to the weekly syndication of her *Design Recipes* articles, which appear in hundreds of newspapers nationwide.

Cathy is known for her keen sense of space, color, and texture, as well as her remarkable ability to effectively envision spaces both for living and for sale.

Home Design Recipes is a robust compilation of hundreds of recipes spanning years of Cathy's designs and installations. The reader is treated to a carefully assembled collection of room-by-room recipes serving as the ultimate DIY guide.

Cathy's concise writing style and practical, easily digestible design advice have been featured in publications such as *O, The Oprah Magazine*, *Redbook*, *Better Homes and Gardens*, *Woman's World*, and *USA Today*, to name a few. Her interior design genius has made her a sought-after expert, frequently appearing on numerous national television programs and online platforms.

Considered an expert at the top of her field, Cathy is a well-respected teacher and mentor. Adept at public speaking and shining on stage, Cathy was chosen as the exclusive interior design talent for Oprah's groundbreaking eight-city "The Life You Want" tour.

After a twenty-year career as a journalist, Cathy transitioned to working full-time as an interior designer, shortly after becoming a finalist on Season 6 of HGTV's hit reality competition series, *Design Star*.

Based in New York City, Cathy's interior design firm, Cathy Hobbs Design Recipes, specializes in real estate staging and styling, vacation and short-term rental design, and residential interior design. Cathy is a popular, trusted "go-to" choice for some of the biggest real estate agents and firms in the New York City tri-state area.

A graduate of one of the top interior design programs in the country, the Fashion Institute of Technology, her commitment and vision is to make interior design approachable and affordable to all who seek the advice and expertise of a professional designer. Cathy also holds a degree in marketing and finance from the University of Southern California.

Cathy splits her time between Brooklyn and New York's Hudson Valley, where she lives with her husband, daughter, and a golden retriever named Buddy.

Find more of Cathy's work at www.cathyhobbs.com. Also, be sure to follow @cathyhobbs and @designrecipes on social media platforms and subscribe to @TheCathyHobbsChannel on YouTube.

CATHY HOBBS

Mango Publishing, established in 2014, publishes an eclectic list of books by diverse authors—both new and established voices—on topics ranging from business, personal growth, women's empowerment, LGBTQ studies, health, and spirituality to history, popular culture, time management, decluttering, lifestyle, mental wellness, aging, and sustainable living. We were named 2019 *and* 2020's #1 fastest growing independent publisher by *Publishers Weekly*. Our success is driven by our main goal, which is to publish high-quality books that will entertain readers as well as make a positive difference in their lives.

Our readers are our most important resource; we value your input, suggestions, and ideas. We'd love to hear from you—after all, we are publishing books for you!

Please stay in touch with us and follow us at:

Facebook: Mango Publishing
Twitter: @MangoPublishing
Instagram: @MangoPublishing
LinkedIn: Mango Publishing
Pinterest: Mango Publishing
Newsletter: mangopublishinggroup.com/newsletter

Join us on Mango's journey to reinvent publishing, one book at a time.